THE NUTS & BOLTS
OF GRANT WRITING

For my mother, Marjorie Ann Carr née Drapela

Hard Work Δ Faith Δ Grace

THE NUTS & BOLTS
OF GRANT WRITING

Cynthia E. Carr

Los Angeles | London | New Delhi
Singapore | Washington DC

Los Angeles | London | New Delhi
Singapore | Washington DC

FOR INFORMATION:

SAGE Publications, Inc.

2455 Teller Road

Thousand Oaks, California 91320

E-mail: order@sagepub.com

SAGE Publications Ltd.

1 Oliver's Yard

55 City Road

London EC1Y 1SP

United Kingdom

SAGE Publications India Pvt. Ltd.

B 1/I 1 Mohan Cooperative Industrial Area

Mathura Road, New Delhi 110 044

India

SAGE Publications Asia-Pacific Pte. Ltd.

3 Church Street

#10-04 Samsung Hub

Singapore 049483

Copyright © 2015 by SAGE Publications, Inc.

Printed in the United States of America

Cataloging-in-Publication data is available from the Library of Congress.

ISBN 978-1-4522-5903-1

This book is printed on acid-free paper.

Publisher: Vicki Knight

Digital Editor: Katie Guarino

Editorial Assistant: Jessica Miller

Production Editor: Olivia Weber-Stenis

Copy Editor: Karin Rathert

Typesetter: C&M Digitals (P) Ltd.

Proofreader: Christine Dahlin

Indexer: Jeanne Busemeyer

Cover Designer: Candice Harman

Marketing Manager: Nicole Elliott

14 15 16 17 18 10 9 8 7 6 5 4 3 2 1

BRIEF CONTENTS

DETAILED CONTENTS

FOREWORD

When I began my term as associate dean some five years ago, I knew little about the world of grants. It was Cynthia Carr, as the grants administrator who worked most closely with our college, who was primarily responsible for my initiation into that world. Cynthia's work with myself and with our faculty led, in that period, to substantial increases in both grants applied for and grants awarded. More faculty than ever before became involved in seeking grants. Junior faculty in particular began their careers with a solid introduction to grantsmanship because of Cynthia's outstanding ability to teach the nuts and bolts of grant seeking.

Cynthia also contributed greatly to establishing a seamless collaboration between the Office of Research and Sponsored Projects, Corporate and Foundation Relations, our Dean's Office, and Post-Award Accounting and Administration. Many problems that would otherwise have arisen at the post-award stage were prevented by Cynthia's careful oversight of the drafting of budgets.

Grant activity is essential to the work of higher education institutions. Grants make it possible for faculty to perform research and scholarship at higher levels because of the time and financial resources they provide for that work. Successful grant applications bring with them increases in institutional reputation and standing. At the same time, even unsuccessful grant applications can benefit an institution over the long term, by ensuring that members of the institution are "at the table" when grant awards are being considered.

Faculty who begin to engage in grant seeking often find that their relationship with their home institution changes for the better as a result, even before one of their applications is successful. Faculty contribute greatly to an institution through their teaching, research, scholarship, creative activity, and service activities. Deans and provosts, along with development professionals, usually bear the burden of finding the resources to fund those activities. Faculty who seek grant funding step into partnership with academic leaders by sharing the burden of finding resources for salaries, fringe benefits, equipment costs, and overhead. Especially in higher education institutions where faculty members are not required to seek grants, academic leaders regard faculty who do so as choosing a higher level of partnership with the institution.

This book offers Cynthia's expertise in grant seeking to faculty who are new to the process. Many department chairs, deans, and provosts will also benefit from reading it, even if they already have a basic understanding of grants. Readers will find in Cynthia not just an experienced and successful grants administrator but most of all a gifted teacher who is adept at communicating her expertise to those who wish to benefit from it.

Jeffrey L. Wilson, PhD

Associate Dean for Faculty and Staff Development and Support

Bellarmine College of Liberal Arts

Loyola Marymount University, Los Angeles

PREFACE

I wrote this book because I love working on grant proposals, and I wanted to share that love with you.

Loving grant proposals may sound odd to some people. Grant proposals are a lot of work. They do not always succeed. Submitting a grant proposal involves working with documents that are not designed to be read for pleasure. The National Institutes of Health's SF424 (R&R) Application Guide, for example, is a very helpful and well-executed document; however, it is no romance novel.

The thing about writing grants is that you can write what is basically a formal academic paper and win money for a deserving project, sometimes a lot of money. Then you use that award to make some small part of the world a better place. That is the grants game for me: the chance to make the world better by using my writing skills.

I have been working with grants for 13 years in various capacities: I have written them, implemented them, performed post-award administration (helping other people run grant projects), as well as providing pre-award services (helping faculty members plan and submit their grants). I have also worked for many different types of colleges and universities, small professional schools, an MA institution, and a research institution. As such, I have a very wide view of grantsmanship that takes in many different institutional situations and ways to conceptualize grant projects.

I wrote this book because although administrators at some institutions may be very enthusiastic about grant seeking and very helpful; however, there may be a lack of infrastructure to assist faculty, students, and staff members as they submit their grant projects. Often this lack of infrastructure manifests as a lack of knowledge: In my experience the most common problem faced by faculty, students, and staff is that they simply do not have the information necessary to submit competitive grants. Some institutions of higher education have elaborate grant mentorship and training programs, but many others do not.

While working with university personnel on grant submissions, I often thought about the thousands of other faculty, students, and staff members who do not have access to the grant writing acumen that my colleagues and I provided. What they needed was a textbook, I thought, or a manual to guide them through the process.

The Nuts and Bolts of Grant Writing, then, was dreamed up as a service to faculty, students, and staff members at institutions of higher education across the United States who are interested in academic grantsmanship but are not quite sure how to begin. I imagined that it would go beyond the standard grant writing book and specifically address the issues faced by the higher education community. It would discuss university bureaucracy and how to navigate it. It would present information on research grants and how to approach the federal government. It would get into the weeds on budgets and submissions and searching. It would provide the opportunity for the beginner to leapfrog over some of the hard lessons that most college and university grant seekers must learn from trial and error.

In writing this book, I am sharing the lessons I learned from working with hundreds of faculty members on their grant projects. They taught me that there are many ways to create a grant proposal within the confines of a funder's guidelines. There are many ways to address reviewer concerns. There are many ways to follow the rules and still present a creative, thoughtful project. When I was a grant writer I thought that I had the one best way to do all this; however, the many faculty members I have worked with showed me that success comes in many forms.

The Nuts and Bolts of Grant Writing features the following chapters:

Chapter 1. Introduction to Grant Seeking

Chapter 2. Grants in the University

Chapter 3. Funders

Chapter 4. Searching

Chapter 5. Project Design

Chapter 6. Budgeting 101

Chapter 7. Traditional Letters of Interest and Proposals

Chapter 8. Grants.gov and Other Online Applications

Chapter 9. Polishing and Formatting the Proposal .

Chapter 10. Declines, Awards, and Grant Administration

This arrangement puts project design first, then budgeting, then writing. This unusual chapter order is the result of watching many different PIs create their grant submissions by trying to design the project and write about it at the same time. Writing a grant proposal before you have designed the project is an unwieldy process.

For this reason, we will first look at project design and the use of a logic model, which can be converted to an outline and then to narrative relatively easily. Taking the budget lines from the logic model will also ensure that the budget and narrative reflect each other appropriately.

While you are using this book and afterward, please feel free to share your experiences and ask questions on the Nuts and Bolts Facebook page: https://www .facebook.com/TheNutsandBoltsofGrantWriting. I would love to hear about your grant writing adventures!

And so, onward!

Cynthia Carr

January 1, 2014

SPECIAL NOTE ON GENDER

Sometimes it is appropriate to use the third-person singular pronoun (he, she) in this book. Rather than using the masculine form exclusively or making all pronouns plural, I have chosen to alternate feminine and masculine pronouns. This means that sometimes you will read "she," and other times you will read "he." Alternation of the genders is impersonal.

ACKNOWLEDGMENTS

I wish to acknowledge the wisdom, assistance, and patience of several people in the making of this book. First of all, I thank the entire SAGE team, especially publisher Vicki Knight, who demonstrated extraordinary patience with me, as well as Katie Guarino, Jessica Miller, Karin Rathert, Santiago Soto, and Olivia Weber-Stenis.

Darcey Whitmore of Loyola Marymount University really helped me bring the project home by reading every written word, correcting many of them, and providing excellent suggestions for improvement. Sara Martinez provided extraordinary help with the illustrations. The following colleagues also provided a great deal of help by reading and commenting on various drafts: Amanda Kay Admire, Dinur Blum, John Carfora, Michaela Curran, Elizabeth Hughes, Julisa McCoy, Alessandro Morosin, and Cynthia Ruiz.

The faculty and staff of the Sociology Department at the University of California, Riverside, displayed great patience and always offered me good advice, particularly Steven G. Brint, Robert A. Hanneman, Richard A. Munoz, Tanya Nieri, Scott V. Savage, and Jan E. Stets.

It is probably not possible to name every person at Loyola Marymount University who helped me improve my skills in grantsmanship, whether through direct transmission of knowledge or through the opportunity to work on projects together. If I worked with you, I thank you!

Joseph C. McNicholas must be particularly mentioned as a mentor and formative influence on my grantsmanship, as well as Joseph Hellige, and Jennifer Abe-Kim, Hawley Almstedt, Elvira Armas, Stephanie August, Anna Bargagliotti, Curtis Bennett, Kristine Brancolini, Stacy Lee Burns, Ann M. Cortez, Karen Mary Davalos, Theresia De Vroom, Jacqueline Dewar, Alice Martini Doyle, Elizabeth Drummond, Sharon Elenbaas, Emily S. Fisher, Véronique Flambard-Weisbart, Judy Foy, James L. Fredericks, Glenn Gebhard, Cecilia González-Andrieu, Victoria Graf, Cheryl Tawede Grills, Catherine F. Grove, Kathleen T. Harris, Mchele Hammers, Anna Harrison, Karen Komosa Hawkins, Dorothea Herreiner, Karen Huchting, Paul W. Humphreys, Robert Hurteau, Paul Jimenez, Nadia Y. Kim, Magaly Lavadenz, Laurie L. Levenson, Holli Levitsky, Stephanie Limoncelli, Edmundo Litton, Chan Lü, Debra J. Martin, Mary McCullough, William P. McKinney,

John Menaghan, Annamaria Muraco, Gene Park, John Michael Parrish, Emma Pastrana, Jeff Phillips, Leslie Ponciano, Luis Proenca, Nigel Raab, Ernest Rose, Gregory Ruzzin, Rebecca Sager, Stephen Shepherd, Todd Charles Shoepe, Richard Shope, Robert Singleton, Daniel L. Smith-Christopher, Eric G. Strauss, Vandana Thadani, David A. Tillipman, Yolanda Uzzell, Robin R. Wang, Michael Waterstone, Jeffrey L. Wilson, Elias Wondimu, Amy Woodson-Boulton, and Thomas Zachariah. This list represents only a few of the many people at LMU to whom I am grateful.

In addition, Michael A. Gottfried of the University of California, Santa Barbara; Chandra L. Muller of the University of Texas, Austin; Philip Nyden of Loyola University, Chicago; and Anne Prisco of Felician College all generously contributed toward this work.

Debbie Winter was my first real grant writing teacher when I worked at the Los Angeles Child Guidance Clinic. I have always remained grateful for all that I learned from her.

I have been fortunate to have a loving and supportive family, not all of whom can be named here. Barrett L. Keller, Douglas and Abbie Carr, Connie Miller Sween, Jennifer Jo, and my son, Pierson J. Bian, have provided stalwart support throughout the development of this book. Connie Marguerite Miller née Larsen and Robert Holden Miller require special mention. They are the parents of the person who made this book possible, my husband Robert R. Miller. Bob made the initial suggestion, urged me to begin writing, and then most generously made space in our home and our relationship for long stretches of writing time. Throughout this path, he has been at my side as a strong supportive force and I cannot imagine a better partner in life.

SAGE Publications and the author would also like to extend a special thanks to the following reviewers for their time and input: Cheryl Winsten-Bartlett, The Art of Science Research Support Services; Janel Bloch, Northern Kentucky University; Jacqueline Dienemann, University of North Carolina, Charlotte; Craig P. Donovan, Kean University; Sandra Yudilevich Espinoza, Salem State University; Tony Filipovitch, Minnesota State University, Mankato; Janet E. Finch, University of Texas at Arlington; Mohammed Forouzesh, California State University, Long Beach; Dana Fredebaugh, Nova Southeastern University; Carol Gettings, State University of New York at Buffalo; Santos H. Hernández, University of Texas at Arlington; Ann Marie LoPrieno, Illinois Institute of Technology; David P. Moxley, University of Oklahoma; David Okech, University of Georgia; Karen A. Randolph, Florida State University; Ratonia C. Runnels, Baylor University; Elizabeth B. Russell, Nazareth College; Diane E. Schmidt, California State University, Chico; Armen Shaomian, University of South Carolina; Sara Smith, University of North Carolina at Chapel Hill; and Olivia Thomas, Portland State University.

ABOUT THE AUTHOR

Cynthia E. Carr has been in service to the higher education community for more than a decade. A successful grant writer and grants administrator, Cynthia has worked at a variety of colleges and universities, including a research institution, an MA institution, and two independent graduate schools. She edited and submitted over 300 grants from 2008 to 2012, resulting in awards from such funders as the National Science Foundation, the National Institutes of Health, the U.S. Department of Education, the U.S. Department of Justice, the John Templeton Foundation, the Robert Wood Johnson Foundation, the John Randolph Haynes and Dora Haynes Foundation, and others.

Cynthia has a continuing interest in research grantsmanship and university structure, both in the United States and internationally. As a Fulbright Specialist awardee, she was invited to consult on higher education fundraising with universities in the Slovak Republic in 2013. Her international interests dovetail with the MA in Islamic Studies she received from UCLA and her extensive travel, particularly in Pakistan and South Korea.

Pursuing her PhD in sociology, Cynthia specializes in higher education stratification, finance, and organizational structure. She also continues to study trends in research grantsmanship and consults with colleges and universities. Cynthia maintains a grant blog on the Nuts and Bolts Facebook page: https://www.facebook.com/TheNutsandBoltsofGrantWriting. Please feel free to visit and join the conversation!

Introduction to Grant Seeking

Welcome to the world of academic grants. Whether you are interested in funding a research project, raising money for community service, applying your math acumen to budgets and grant accounts, or simply putting your good writing skills to use, there is a place for you in university grant seeking.

Universities raise millions, even billions of dollars, every year in research and program grants from various levels of government and thousands of U.S. foundations. For example, in 2012 Johns Hopkins University reported the highest amount of research and development expenditures of any U.S. university at $2,106,185,000. Eighty-eight percent of this work was funded by U.S. federal agencies, and about 5.42% of it was funded by nonprofit organizations, including foundations (National Center for Science and Engineering Statistics, 2014). This type of funding is acquired primarily through grant writing and contracts.

In other words, Johns Hopkins was awarded research and development funds through the preparation of planning documents (proposals) to perform specific work for a specific amount of funding, and the expenditure of these awarded monies added up to more than $2 billion in 2010.

Many people work together to create this kind of financial value, which translates into important research and community work that build up the university as well as the wider society. Hardworking university grant seekers include principal investigators (PIs), postdoctoral workers, grants administrators, grant accountants, department personnel, foundation and corporate officers, and graduate students. They fulfill many different roles in grant seeking and administration. Although we will talk about PIs a great deal, it is important to keep in mind that grant seeking is a team endeavor and everyone's contribution is important to winning an award.

For now we will consider a more foundational question: What is a grant?

Box 1.1   Your Project

What are your fundraising goals? Are you interested in research or in building projects to help your institution and the community? If you could make up and run a project, what would it be? How would the project serve the community? Keep these ideas in mind as you read.

WHAT IS A GRANT, AND WHY WOULD I WRITE ONE?

People do not actually write grants; they write grant proposals. A **grant proposal** is a document composed to describe a project and ask for funding to implement it. The proposal includes a vision for the project, the work to be done, how much money is needed, and what outcomes are expected. If the proposal offers a good idea, is written clearly, responds to the funder's request, and the PI is lucky, a grant of money (or other resources) may be made to further the project. The organization that awards the resources is called the **funder.** In the academic context, the person responsible for the proposal, especially when it is a scholarly or scientific pursuit, is called the PI. In academic grants, the PI normally works for a university or college, which acts as steward or guardian of the funds. As such, the monies generally go to the institution and are ultimately under the institution's **stewardship** or control. A **fellowship** is a special type of grant that may go directly to the PI and tends to support his or her time and personal research expenses. Many graduate student grant awards are actually fellowships.

Of course, colleges and universities are made up of many different departments that represent various disciplines and interest areas. Each of these has its own traditions and styles of writing, including grant writing. This book will therefore concentrate on the basic and applied social sciences: anthropology, economics, political science, psychology, sociology, and of course, education (including science education, K–12, and higher education).

This book, *The Nuts and Bolts of Grant Writing*, is dedicated to assisting you with your pursuit of grants in the academic context. Although there are many good books that teach grant writing, grants at colleges and universities need the specific treatment this book offers for several reasons.

WHAT MAKES ACADEMIC GRANTS DIFFERENT?

Colleges, universities, and professional schools form unique work environments dedicated to intellectual activity.

Although they are primarily organized around the most basic service they provide, educating students, higher education institutions also create value through research and scholarship. In other words, unlike the average company, which creates and sells widgets, or the average nonprofit, which provides a specific service to a population, colleges and universities create and disseminate knowledge in a wide variety of ways. Grants are a distinctive part of this complex organizational, intellectual, and business process and they require special treatment.

The Nuts and Bolts of Grant Writing *is specifically dedicated to providing firsthand, practical information about grants at colleges, universities, and independent graduate schools.*

Colleges and universities have specialized organizational structures around grant seeking that are unique to the academic field.

Some of these structures include **sponsored projects offices**, post award offices, **corporate and foundation relations (CFR)** offices, and so forth. Becoming effective at university grant seeking often requires the ability to navigate an internal organizational environment that is unknown in other parts of the nonprofit world.

Beginning with Chapter 2, specific hands-on information on how to deal with grant-related university offices will be included.

Many (although not all) personnel at universities write grants to fund research projects.

Research is a distinctive and specific type of grant writing with unique considerations, concerns, and funders. *The Nuts and Bolts of Grant Writing* concentrates on research grants and the types of service grants academic personnel are most likely to develop and submit.

All chapters of this book feature extended discussions of research grants and how they differ from service grants. Differences between research funders and service funders (often foundations) will also be discussed.

University academic personnel have a great deal of freedom to submit grant proposals; however, they do not always receive guidance on marketable ideas and project development.

While research universities do provide mentorship and guidance for grant seekers, there are thousands of colleges and universities with primarily teaching missions and a growing expectation that faculty and staff will engage in grant seeking. These institutions often offer few resources to assist PIs as they begin grant development.

While this book cannot replace a mentor, it is designed to assist academic personnel and graduate students who may not have access to immediate grant-seeking guidance and/or mentorship.

In Chapter 2, we will discuss grants in higher education more extensively.

PROPOSAL DEVELOPMENT WILL CHANGE YOUR CAREER

The discipline associated with regular proposal development will change the way you think in important ways and create positive change in other areas of your work life—if you engage in it seriously. Effective proposal development requires not only grant writing but also project management: idea development, team leadership, financial analysis, and strong organizational skills. As a function of grant writing, many faculty and staff members even create their own small service and research offices within their schools. In effect, they become the heads of subunits, and they serve as leaders and managers as well as researchers.

In the beginning of the grant-seeking process, the task is grant writing. As soon as you win a grant, however, the task becomes project management. Here are four ways that grant writing will change your perspective:

1. **Grant seekers learn to evaluate project ideas in terms of their appeal to outside audiences.**

   It is often not enough to have a good idea; in order to get a project going, you must convince other people that it is a good idea. Experienced PIs learn to look at ideas in terms of their potential appeal to various audiences. They also learn how to present these ideas in compelling ways.

   Effective leaders must learn to evaluate ideas in terms of their "marketability" for internal audiences and external stakeholders as they are planning organizational change, new programs, and so forth. Capable leaders must master the art of persuasion.

2. **Grant seekers learn to work in teams.**

     Most grant proposals are created by colleagues working together. Team grant writing requires some finesse because each individual will have different ideas, writing styles, and work styles. An academic grants team often works with a variety of offices populated with people who may have very different ideas about how grants should be created and administered. Faculty team members at other universities also bring different institutional perspectives. Successful PIs learn how to lead a team of colleagues with diverse outlooks and histories toward the submission and eventual administration of grant projects.

     Managers in a variety of fields must also develop leadership skills to keep work processes moving forward, organized, and promptly completed yet maintain a positive work environment.

3. **Grant seekers learn to explain administrative matters clearly.**

     As part of a grant proposal, a PI must write clear plans about how she will use grant money to conduct activities that help accomplish larger goals. She must balance the minutiae with a visionary goal in ways that will convince reviewers that she has a handle on every level of detail: What are the steps involved in establishing a research center? How does one go about creating a new dataset or conducting a national survey? The PI must set out a clear, cogent work plan based on the available budget.

     Directors and chairs must also learn to express their plans in writing. They must articulate the details of work processes for strategic plans, department goal setting, and organizational reporting for a variety of audiences.

4. **Grant seekers begin to think in terms of what is possible to accomplish, and this translates into a budget.**

     They develop a sense of what can be accomplished by a certain number of people with a specific type of training within specific time constraints working within the unique context of their institutions. For example, they naturally begin to estimate how many graduate students it will take at 20 hours per week to conduct 100 interviews or how many hours a week they will need an administrative assistant to help with project management.

     Chairs and directors must also develop the ability to estimate the resources they need to accomplish the tasks of their department or office, whether the resources are personnel, spatial configurations, or the number of filing cabinets that need to be ordered for the new filing system.

THE PARTS OF A GRANT PROPOSAL

Every grant proposal is different; however, most of them are composed of four basic elements: a fundable idea, a narrative, a budget, and sundry documentation. All of these are created with the guidance of the funder, usually through a set of instructions called **guidelines** or a **request for proposals (RFP).**

Every funded grant starts with a great idea; however, not every great idea is fundable. Figuring out whether your idea has a chance of success takes some experience and some practice. One way to begin building such experience is to run some grant searches (which we will go over in Chapter 4) just to survey funders and get a sense of what sorts of projects they are interested in. An argument can be made that it is better to survey what types of funding are available before the grant seeker begins to form his idea. This is a very practical way to begin the grant-seeking process, and I recommend it

You can also talk to advisors, mentors, and trusted colleagues with grant experience about what they see as fundable. Disciplinary conferences, which are often attended by representatives of both foundations and federal agencies, are great places to get information. Attending a presentation by **program officers** (professional foundation and government agency staff) will give you an immediate sense of programs and expectations. You can usually approach program officers and agency representatives after the presentation and ask them questions. In this way you can get immediate feedback on the potential fundability of an idea.

The following are a few attributes of a fundable idea.

Fundable ideas are often practical and will accomplish something useful.

Funders usually like to put their money toward something that will accomplish tangible goals. Even with research, the ultimate goal of the project will be to ascertain the usefulness of a methodology or to discover the links between a potential cause and effect in order to make it available for implementation to help people.

Awarded ideas may help solve a known problem.

Often enough work has already been done by various scholars or programs so that the direction of the solution is already known. If it is a research project, the idea has some literature behind it, and if it is a service project, the idea often incorporates recognized best practice methods.

Awarded ideas are generally described in detail.

While there are funders, such as the National Science Foundation (NSF), who are interested in bench or theoretical science, even here an exploratory study will be conducted in a specific and predefined area. Prep work (like other similar studies or a pilot project) is often expected for research proposals. True exploratory projects where the end result is completely unknown are unusual.

Successful ideas are usually measurable.

The results of the project will be based on the measurement of some aspect of reality, whether this is people's opinions, the rate of incarceration, or how many research articles universities produce. Measurable results drive conclusions forward more effectively and are often more attractive to funders.

Fundable ideas are generally the next logical step.

Simply filling the gaps in literature does not make for great grant ideas, yet many times a funded idea feels like the next logical step in a disciplinary process: Where has your discipline been lately, and where is it headed? Sometimes a funded idea is simply in the right place at the right time in terms of the current thinking.

Finally, for both research and service projects go to the literature. If a question has already been thoroughly answered, you probably will not be funded to answer it again. Similarly, if an idea is too far ahead of current research, this may lead to declines as well. A fundable idea often falls somewhere between obvious and daring, a space that is different for each discipline and changes over time.

Be on top of new discoveries and know the current methodologies of your discipline. You will also need to both prove why you have chosen your methods and make predictions about how well your plans will work. If your techniques are based on stale literature, peer reviewers will know it. If there is an important item that you have left out, they will notice. If you avoid dealing with major controversies, they may think you are unaware of them and therefore not up to date on the literature.

Narrative

The **narrative**, a textual description of the project, is the most familiar part of the proposal for most people. Grant narratives can run from half a page for some online applications to 50 pages for some federal competitions. Proposal narratives are most often written in standard nonfiction, third-person voice with words that are as complex as required to do the job of description.

Grant narratives can also be called project descriptions, and some funders break the narrative down into smaller sections, like "Background," "Need for Project," "Project Description," "Methodology," "Sustainability," and so forth. In this book when narrative is mentioned, it will indicate all the written, descriptive parts of the proposal. In later chapters, we will delve into the style and organization of a well-written narrative and demonstrate how this process can be enhanced by the accomplishment of sound ancillary tasks, like the use of logic models and the creation of a strong budget.

Budget

The budget is often left to complete last, and yet it is quite literally the backbone of all projects. A poorly completed budget will kill a project, if not in review then in implementation. Poor budgets lead to bad projects, which can lead to problems with the funder and/or problems with your institution.

Beginning PIs often misunderstand the significance of the budget. It is not just another exercise required to effect a submission. The budget is the translation of the project into financial language, the language of the controller's office, or accounting, or whoever handles the organization's books, pays the bills, and signs the checks.[1] The budget is the thing that allows the PI to be sure there is enough money to pay incentives to participants, rent the van to pick up the advisory board, buy validated survey instruments, or buy a round-trip ticket to the archive.

In most cases, the **budget** is a list of items **(lines)** on a spreadsheet with the cost in a separate column to allow for summing (see Figure 1.1). The budget may be broken down into several sections, and the guidelines may call for a **budget narrative or justification:** a written explanation for each item requested. Each institution participating in a project will have a specific, unique budget. In this book *budget* will refer to all budget-related documents for any particular proposal.

A sound budget is a beautiful thing, and it is hoped that this book will help new PIs appreciate the centrality of the budget to a well-executed project.

Sundry Documentation

There are other items that may need to be acquired, created, and submitted with a proposal, and these will be listed in the RFP or in the guidelines. Some of these items will be quite easy to find, while others will seem nearly impossible. Sometimes the PI should begin planning immediately to acquire specific items. Results will vary; however, below is a non-exhaustive example

---

[1] I have heard this sentiment attributed to Patricia Hawk, the Director of the Office of Sponsored Programs at Oregon State University.

Figure 1.1 Example Budget

A	B	C	D	E	F	G	H	J
1			Working (Internal) Budget					
2			**Bob Miller, Sociology**					
3			Teaching STEM Subjects in Introductory University Courses (TSUIC)					
4			NSF REESE					
5			Deadline: July 17					
6								
7			*Item*			*6/1/2013–5/31/2014*	*6/1/2014–5/31/2015*	*Total*
8			**1. Senior Personnel (All salaries subject to 2% rise per year)**					
9			A. Bob Miller, PI, 2 months summer effort	$82,440	2	$18,320	$18,686	$37,006
10			B. Mahmud Jamal, Co-PI, 15% effort (1 course remission per year)	$76,780	.15	$11,517	$11,747	$23,264
11			C. Mahmud Jamal, Co-PI, 1 month summer effort	$76,780	1	$8,531	$8,702	$17,233
12			D. Chandra Simms, Statistician, 2 weeks summer effort	$95,101	1	$5,283	$5,389	$10,672
13			**Subtotal Senior Personnel**			**$43,652**	**$44,525**	**$88,176**

This example working budget is a snapshot of the budget we will be examining in Case Study 2.

list of commonly requested items, ranked loosely from relatively easy to very difficult for the average PI to acquire:

- Organizational mission
- PI list of current and pending grants, biographical sketch[2]
- Tax forms or 990s
- Organizational budget
- Collaborators' biographical sketches, current and pending grants, budgets, and narratives
- College, department, or office budget
- Presidential signature
- List of pending grants across the institution
- Board chair signature
- Board vote on submission

As defined by the funder, the narrative is composed of all written elements; the budget is composed of all financial elements; and the sundry documentation, altogether, comprise the grant proposal.

HOW DO I GET A GRANT AND KEEP IT?

The answer to this question comes in three words: Follow the directions.

The directions are an intrinsic part of grant writing and are most often represented as the RFP or the guidelines.[3] Foundations most often present guidelines (often found on the official website), and federal funders generally issue RFPs.

PIs that ignore the funder's directions are at a high risk of wasting their time: In many cases, the funder's staff will only send correctly developed proposals to reviewers. Even in the case when an incorrectly developed proposal is passed on for review, reviewers are often given a rubric based on the RFP or guidelines to help them evaluate the submissions. A PI who has not created the proposal according to the directions, therefore, also risks losing substantial points, and this generally results in a decline.

---

[2]The National Science Foundation (NSF) and National Institutes of Health (NIH) both require biographical sketches (or bio sketches) in lieu of CVs.

[3]In addition, there may be other labels, such as RFQ (Request for Qualifications) or RFA (Request for Applications). A sense of determination may be required to find all instructions from some funders.

Box 1.2   Grant-Seeking Tip

The RFP or guidelines tell the PI the following:

- Exactly what sections should be prepared
- Formatting, including font, font size, margins, line spacing
- Page limits for each section
- Which items can be included in the budget request
- The maximum amount of money that can be requested

RFPs and guidelines certainly do contribute to the tediousness of the grant writing process. An RFP can include 150 pages of direction, guidance, mission, background, and so forth, perhaps well organized and concise, perhaps repetitive and poorly organized. RFPs do not display humor, sparkling prose, or profound philosophical thinking: They are administrative documents. Yet the time spent dealing with these documents will reap a more competitive proposal and is therefore well worth the investment.

A Grant Is Like a Contract

A grant proposal is a promise to carry out a specific project, and as such, it can be legally binding. The true contractual nature of the relationship becomes apparent when an award is made by the funder and accepted by the institution: This often involves signed documents. The funder will expect that anything promised in the proposal will be completed by the PI and/or the institution. For example, a proposal to study a methadone clinic in Boise will need to be implemented at a methadone clinic in Boise, not Pocatello. Normally major **post-award** changes (or changes made after the award has been accepted) can only be made after consultation with the funder.

What happens if you do not spend a grant out according to plan or if it looks as if the PI has a **conflict of interest** (meaning that she could stand to illicitly benefit from the grant work)? The funder has the right to take the money back. This includes all the money, the entire grant, even the parts that were spent correctly. It is therefore possible to spend out two years ($200,000) of a three-year ($300,000) grant and have the funder request the money back if the work is not progressing, has been misspent, or a significant conflict of interest emerges.

This situation happens regularly, as described, for example, in the yearly NSF Inspector General Reports to Congress (available on the NSF website, search for Office of Inspector General). For example, in March 2012, the NSF Inspector General wrote:

> Our investigations have recovered nearly $1.4 million from those who fraudulently sought to obtain funds intended for scientific research. We continue to aggressively pursue cases of research misconduct which undermines citizens' trust in government-funded research and referred eight research misconduct cases to NSF. (Office of Inspector General, 2012)

This wording, "fraudulently sought to obtain funds," does not necessarily mean that those who wrote the proposals in question were consciously seeking to deceive the NSF. One of the institutions cited in the report was noted for having weak internal controls (ineffective internal financial policies and procedures). It is entirely possible that the PI did not know his institution had weak internal controls, and yet the funds for that grant were taken back by the NSF. The point here is that noncompliance can lead to unpleasant consequences, even for the PIs who are careful about conflicts of interest, do not plagiarize, and spend out their grants properly.

THE GRANT LIFE CYCLE

The grant life cycle spirals between activities as the proposal is prepared and sent out, declines or awards are received, and projects are implemented and closed out. Figure 1.2 illustrates the spiral nature of grant seeking.

Preparing the Proposal (1–7)

This process is the substantial work of grant writing and forms the primary content of this book. Preparing the proposal begins with a great idea (1) and the search for a funder (2). Once a funder has been found, it then continues into all the sundry tasks designed to explicate the project in line with the instructions of the funder, including development of research questions or project goals (3), using your logic model to design the project (4), creating a budget (5), developing the narrative (6), getting feedback on the narrative (7), and ending up with the first submission (8). This process can take four months when working on a large multiyear project with partners, but it can also be belted out in four weeks. Proposals can also be written and delivered in two weeks; however, a two-week investment of work is often quite obvious to reviewers.

Figure 1.2   The Grant Life Cycle

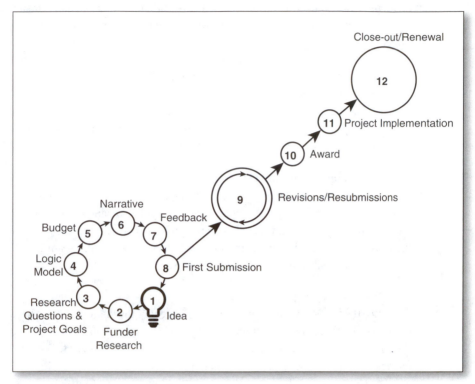

The grant life cycle includes multiple iterations of proposal submissions as well as renewals.

Submission (8)

Submission (8) is accomplished through a variety of systems, including online, email, and by post (post office submission is getting more and more rare, however). Inexperienced PIs may discount the submission process, thinking it will be quick—just the press of a button. Submission is never really a fast process, however, especially if you take the time to check things over carefully. As part of a proper submission process, errors will emerge that can drag the process out interminably, potentially resulting in a missed deadline. It is best, therefore, to give three days to the submission process. When a submission goes awry, this time cushion can save the day.

Decline/Award (9, 10)

First submissions are often (although not always) declined, and the next stage is revisions and resubmissions (9), hopefully not too many, until you are awarded

(10). Declines can be very frustrating; however, they are common, and for most people they are a necessary part of the learning curve. Declines from federal competitions often come with reviewer comments. Although it can be emotionally trying, these comments are extremely important to refining a project and are often a boon to one's grant writing skills. Successful PIs study reviewer comments.

On the other hand, if the PI is awarded, she is well advised to take some time to celebrate. The real work, running the project, will begin shortly! This happy time, the new award period, is often heralded by a negotiation process where the PI may be asked to cut 20 percent from her budget. As soon as the celebration party is over, she calls the sponsored projects office and rolls up her sleeves to begin the next stage.

Project Implementation (11)

Once awarded, the PI moves into project implementation (11), also known as grant administration. This phase begins when money or a convincing award letter arrives and the PI may begin spending on the project, depending on the policy of the institution. As much work as the proposal may appear to take, grant implementation is actually the most work-intensive part of the process.

Closeout and Reapplication (12)

Once the funds have been spent out and, hopefully, the grant objectives have been accomplished, the closeout process begins (12). As the PI sits down to write the "final" report, it may or may not be the true end of the project. Different funders may provide renewals, reapplications, no-cost extensions, and the like, allowing some projects to live long, useful lives. When and how to make the next approach will be on the PI's mind as he or she begins this process again.

Box 1.3   Three Steps to a Great Submission

1. Follow directions.

2. Follow directions!

3. FOLLOW DIRECTIONS!!

ONWARD

External funding can make a dream project a reality, it can jumpstart a career, and it can create additional value in a tenure portfolio. Further, an award of funding, no matter the size, is a vote of confidence in your thinking and planning. It is an award on the basis of work accomplished. It is professional validation. I have always thought of grant awards as honor and glory, both for the grant seeker and for the institution, but then I am a very enthusiastic person.

Box 1.4 True Story

I was once associated with an underspent grant from a city. The PI had worked extensively with the NSF, which is rather generous with grant extensions, and so perhaps from habit, she did not worry about the pace of her spending. When the end of the grant period rolled around, her grant budget was underspent by about $25,000. With confidence, she asked the city for an extension to continue the work.

This PI was astonished to hear that not only was her request for an extension refused but the rest of the grant was forfeited. Because the grant was paid out as receipts were turned in, money did not have to be returned; however, the university considered that this PI had lost thousands of dollars by not spending the grant according to the proposal.

Grant development and the work that emerges from grant awards can enlarge your horizon, your potential, your track record, your success, and your list of good deeds accomplished. The grants world is a new world to explore. It is waiting for you to discover, to try, to test yourself, to enlarge your skill set, to increase your scope of competence, to win honor and glory, and to submit a proposal. Who knows? Maybe your idea will get awarded, and you will be off creating the next new thing to save humankind, your local school, or a child.

THE NUTS & BOLTS

Here are a few of the general ideas I hope you took from this chapter.

1. An awarded grant proposal becomes a type of contract in which the PI uses grant funds to perform specific tasks, usually research or services.

2. Some items of a proposal may take longer to acquire or create than others; therefore PIs should carefully evaluate what is required for submission before beginning work.

3. The most important thing PIs need to keep in mind when grant writing is to FOLLOW DIRECTIONS.

4. The grant life cycle at the university moves from preparation to submission to decline/award to administration to closeout and/or reapplication.

EXERCISES: WORKING TOWARD MASTERY

1. Write an essay on your own interest in grants. What project are you interested in getting funded? What do you imagine you will accomplish as a result of a grant award? (Write a minimum of one page.)

2. As you look over this essay, what challenges do you foresee in pursuing this project? Do not forget to consider all the potential pitfalls that might be involved: narrative production (writing), budget production (planning and math), availability of funders, methodology issues, facilities, institutional challenges, explanatory issues, and so forth. (Write a minimum of one page.)

CHAPTER TERMS

Budget: A list of items (lines) typically on a spreadsheet with the cost in a separate column to allow for summing.

Budget narrative or justification: A document that features a brief narrative on each line of the budget explaining the need for the item and the method of estimation used to arrive at the amount requested.

CFR (corporate and foundation relations): The university department or office that oversees nonresearch foundation proposals and awards. CFR is part of advancement or university relations.

Conflict of interest: A situation in which a party stands to gain inappropriately from a grant or contract. For example, a PI who had received conference funding from a pharmaceutical company might be considered to have a conflict of interest if he was awarded a grant to carry on clinical trials of that company's new product.

Fellowship: A type of grant often made directly to the faculty member or graduate student to fund time, travel, or other scholarly activities.

Funder: A foundation, government agency, affinity group, or other entity offering grant awards for specific types of research or service.

Grant proposal: A document composed to describe a project for which funding is requested.

Guidelines: Instructions issued by a funder to guide the development of a proposal.

Lines or line items: Items included and costs in a budget. Such items are listed vertically, down the lines of the spreadsheet.

Narrative: All of the project description sections submitted as one document.

PI (principal investigator): The lead investigator on a grant, usually holding authority as the responsible party for grant management.

Post-award: The grants process after an award has been made and/or the individuals who assist the PI with the implementation of the grant.

Program officer: A professional foundation or government agency staff member involved in the grants process.

RFP (request for proposals): A document issued by a government agency or foundation that details a funding opportunity, including the content and format of proposal submissions.

SPO (sponsored projects office), academic grants: The office in a college or university that oversees the submission and often the administration of external grant awards primarily for research.

Stewardship: In fundraising, the careful management of funds or resources given by a funder to the institution (steward) for a specific purpose. Part of stewardship is reporting back regularly to the funder on the disposition of funds and project progress.

2

Grants in the University

INTRODUCTION

The word *grant* is rather magical in an institution of higher education. It indicates that money is coming in from outside to accomplish research (the coin of the university realm), a service project, or an institutional objective, like new construction or a scholarship program. When a college or university wins a grant, particularly a large one, the institution is validated in several ways:

- The funder believes in the work of the institution. This is particularly true when the grant comes from a foundation. Giving a grant of money and thereby associating the name of the foundation with the college or university is a great public validation for the school.
- The funder believes in the work of the principal investigator (PI). Research grants are one way of validating the intellectual work of the faculty in a public way. They confer confidence in the work of the PI, and therefore of the department, office, school, and ultimately the entire institution.
- External funding often leads to exciting new developments. A college or university with a number of grant projects may be on the leading edge of research in these areas, thereby boosting institutional visibility further.
- The more research grants a college or university receives, the more likely it is to receive more grants. Success and validation tend to lead to more success and validation in a virtuous cycle.

For these and many other reasons, your college, university, or professional school will probably be very supportive of your efforts to win a grant award.

This chapter provides an introduction to those aspects of grant seeking that are specific to the academic environment. It involves the definition of many specific terms that will be used throughout the rest of the book.

Box 2.1 The Nuts & Bolts: Do Grants Earn an Institution "Profit" Through the Indirect Cost Rate?

The universities, colleges, and independent graduate schools discussed in this book are all nonprofit organizations, so no "profit" is earned as a result of any financial process that they are involved in.

The **indirect cost rate** or overhead is a percentage of the direct costs of a project added on to the total grant request to pay for the share of expenses, such as electricity, building maintenance, libraries, accounting infrastructure, and so forth, which are hard to measure (more on this in Chapter 6). As such, indirect costs represent the estimated costs of running the institution so that the project can take place.

The full indirect cost rate is not always paid out for each grant. For this and other reasons, the total indirect cost rate probably only comes close to covering the actual cost of research for high-end research universities. Most other schools end up subsidizing grants in various ways.

THE VARIETIES OF PI

In some institutions (like research universities) and for some disciplines, writing grants is a given, and there are grant-awarded PIs in nearly every department. Different disciplines have different needs for and access to grant funding, however. Below is a list of the groups who tend to submit grants from the average college or university and how they may think of and pursue external funding:

- Science, technology, engineering and mathematics (**STEM**) researchers: For many of these fields, research cannot be conducted without extra funds, or it cannot be conducted on a scale large enough to make a difference in the extension of knowledge. Because discoveries in these disciplines often spin off into commercial and governmental applications, there are many grant opportunities for the "hard" sciences from both government and private sources.

- Social scientists: On the other hand, social scientists do not always feel they must pursue grants because their research may or may not be expensive enough to require external funding. In some cases, adequate research can be conducted by a faculty member on sabbatical. Grant funding may be quite important to creating a major dataset, conducting a national survey, or engaging in long-term qualitative fieldwork, however.

- Education faculty: Grant support is a mainstay of many education faculty members because educational research is often applied and may consist of measuring the effect of various interventions on students in the classroom. When done correctly this kind of research tends to be fairly expensive. Several agencies in the federal government (in addition to the U.S. Department of Education) and many foundations offer grant funding for educational research on every level of K–12, and at the university.

- Faculty in the humanities: Fellowships are a mainstay of a humanities faculty. Fellowships are grants primarily made to enhance institutional funding of research time during a sabbatical or for the summer. Of course, there are humanities faculty members who win larger awards, including from the National Endowment for the Humanities.

- Staff members: Staff members also submit grant proposals for a variety of reasons. Sometimes they work in research labs and so are assisting PIs with applications for external funding. Sometimes they work in corporate and foundation relations offices and submit grants on behalf of the institution. Other times, specific university departments, like a medical or psychological clinic or the office of diversity, may be very involved in grant seeking to augment university services.

At most brick and mortar universities, there is an office or department of advancement, **development,** or university relations, and I will refer to these collectively as development, since this is their traditional name and still indicates their essential fundraising responsibility. Development officers may write grant proposals to fund buildings, scholarships, and large (non-research-based) mission-critical programs. Anyone writing grants at a university will probably run into development staff at some point, so although this book will tend to be limited to research and service grants of non-development faculty and staff, mention will be made of the places where these faculty and staff grant seekers may cross paths with development personnel.

> ## Box 2.2   Use of URLs in This Book
>
> When I refer to websites in this book, I will give the main URL and then suggest search terms. This is because websites and URLs can change very quickly, while this book will remain the same until the next edition. I want you to be able to find the information in the most effective way possible, and that often will mean a search of the website using key terms.

TYPES OF ACADEMIC GRANTS

Generally for faculty and staff, there are three main types of grants at an institution of higher education: research grants, fellowships, and service grants.

Research Grants

A research grant is built around research questions and includes a full description of the methodology involved in the investigation. The results of a research grant are usually fairly well hypothesized in advance: The investigation is couched in related literature that gives the reviewer a sense of anticipated results and/or the PI may be expected to have already carried out a pilot project or related investigation.

Research grants are not made to provide services to the local university community but to explore and gain knowledge about some aspect of the world. For social scientists, some research grants are designed around a community intervention; however, such projects are not generally put in place as permanent community programs but as investigations. Research grants are often tied to the discipline of the PI and will feature specific disciplinary assumptions, literature, and methodology.

Research grants feature descriptions of how the PI will conduct the investigation according to disciplinary research guidelines and may require human subjects review by **the institutional review board (IRB)**. While service grants are open to some amount of "tweaking" to get the program right as it is molded to community needs, research grants normally do not have this flexibility. Because the intervention methodology defines the quality of the research conducted, it must be followed exactly.

Although there is strong federal involvement in research grant making, there are also many foundations that regularly fund research or that might be interested in specific research projects that are strongly related to the foundation mission.

Fellowships

A fellowship is a special type of grant that is designed to provide funding in three general situations. Fellowships can fund the following:

- Faculty members on sabbatical usually receive one half year (one semester) of sabbatical funding that the faculty member can choose to take as one semester at full salary or as a full year at half salary. Many fellowships are designed to provide about one half year of salary so that the faculty member can combine this with the reduced sabbatical salary and spend a full year on research.
- Funds for humanities research, including visits to archives, libraries, scholarly travel, stays at dedicated scholarly institutions, and so forth.
- Graduate students to further their studies, by funding tuition, stipend or research expenses.

Service Grants

University faculty and staff may seek grants to help provide services to students or for the community surrounding their institutions. For example, many such grant competitions are provided by the U.S. Department of Education in order to bolster the educational attainment of underserved groups. Trio programs, which "serve and assist low-income individuals, first-generation college students, and individuals with disabilities to progress through the academic pipeline" (U.S. Department of Education, 2011), are a good example of federal funding to universities that benefit the surrounding community.

University PIs can apply for grants to provide a wide variety of services—for example, mental health services, consumer finance training, to assist local schools with instruction or afterschool programs, to create science education programs, and so forth.

TYPES OF AWARDS

College and university faculty generally make a distinction between two types of award processes: peer-reviewed and non-peer-reviewed. The difference becomes important in terms of tenure portfolios and academic respect. Winning a peer-reviewed grant is generally considered a more challenging and intellectually important thing to do.

Peer-Reviewed Awards

The process of peer-reviewed granting works much like that of peer-reviewed journal articles. The funder will invite noncompeting faculty to read the submitted proposals for a particular grant competition and rate them for research quality (see diagram below), perhaps by using a rubric. The funding agency will then often set a cut line at the point that reflects the number of awards to be made or amount of money available to distribute for the competition. Proposals ranked

Figure 2.1   The Award Cut-Off Line in an NIH-Style Competition

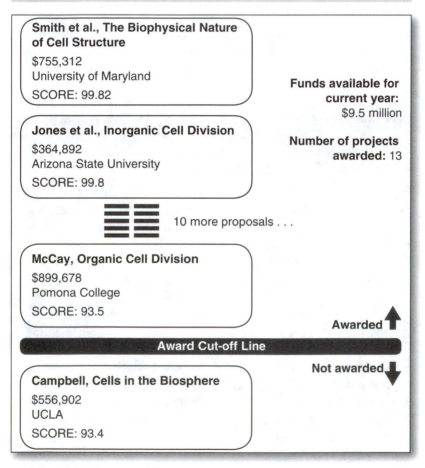

Note the tenth of a point difference of score between the funded project with the lowest score and the unfunded project with the highest score. This is why attention to detail is so important: Funding can be won or lost by a tenth of a point, depending on the competition.

above the line will get funded, the rest will be declined. See Figure 2.1 for a conceptual example of the cut-off line in an NIH-style competition.

Federal funders often make peer-reviewed awards—for example, the National Science Foundation (NSF), National Institutes of Health (NIH), National Institute of Justice and U.S. Department of Education, among others.

Non-Peer-Reviewed Awards

These competitions are often decided by program officers in a federal agency or the board of directors at a foundation. The small number of foundations established to fund academic research may use peer review; however, foundations are generally run by philanthropists and their staff rather than by academics. Funding is therefore awarded by philanthropists, often sitting on the board of directors, or by foundation staff members. This results in a decidedly nonacademic reputation for foundation awards in many departments and at many institutions.

Box 2.3 The Nuts & Bolts: Predominantly Undergraduate Institutions

Comprehensive or master's institutions and liberal arts colleges are very different types of institutions; however, they can be considered together for some aspects of grant preparation. What these two institution types share is a dedication to teaching undergraduate students (as well as research and service), and I include them in one group when I refer to **predominantly undergraduate institutions (PUIs)**. There was a time when faculty in these types of universities were not expected to perform much in the way of research; however, for faculty at many of these institutions, the pressure to accomplish solid research has grown (Youn and Price, 2009; Mal-achowski, 2003). For example, even in PUIs, publications, not teaching, accounts for most pay raises despite the fact that liberal arts colleges and comprehensives tend to be dedicated to pedagogy (Fairweather, 2005).

There are rarely department-level grants administrators at PUIs; most of the action occurs in the central sponsored projects office. The good news is that the central sponsored projects office at a PUI is often a very different resource from what is found at research universities. When a PUI is consciously trying to increase grants, the institution may staff these offices with former grant writers or even former academics with a professional interest in grantsmanship.

GRANT SEEKING AT DIFFERENT TYPES OF INSTITUTIONS

Faculty and staff members from any type of institution of higher education can write a proposal and be awarded a grant for research, student development, or community service. The key is to understand the institution, create a program that fits with its mission and financial capacity, and match this with funder requirements. Grants management infrastructure and acumen tend to expand as the institution grows.

Community colleges are not always thought of first when people think about grants; however, community colleges are prime vehicles for outreach to under-served populations and first generation college students, an important community for many U.S. Department of Education programs. Community colleges have also become de facto trade schools (Eighmy, 2009) and as such can garner important grants from federal and state agencies and corporate or industry groups interested in creating opportunity for workers across the occupational spectrum. While the grants will often be driven by administrators rather than faculty, the community college is an excellent place for those interested in frontline assistance to underserved students through grant projects.

Comprehensives or master's institutions often strongly encourage faculty to apply for grants; however, grant assistance and experienced help for PIs are not always readily available. Patience and good teamwork may be particularly necessary to develop grants when the PI is new to grantsmanship and when grants are a fairly new item on campus.

Liberal arts colleges are very similar to comprehensives in this matter. Although pressure has increased to win grants and awards, the institutional capacity to assist faculty to acquire and manage them is not always available. Elite liberal arts colleges may have a wealth of assistance; however, results will be variable for other institutions.

Nonprofit professional graduate schools often compete for grants from local foundations to build institutional capacity and provide new programs, especially community service programs. Professional graduate schools tend to follow a nonprofit model of grant seeking and rarely compete for research grants.

Research universities generally have robust research programs and are very competitive in the grants arena. Research universities have earned their designation: Creating new knowledge is an important part of their mission, and the importance of grant writing is not overlooked on these campuses. Faculty members at research universities often have a great deal of grants experience and expertise, and many have large labs with postdoctoral staff and graduate students working away at their research projects and grants.

Many research universities feature local department-level grants administrators as well as the central sponsored projects office. Depending on the institution, the department administrator may be a part of sponsored projects or may be supervised from within the department. When I refer to sponsored projects, therefore, readers from research universities should be thinking about their go-to academic grant administrator, whether this is a department-level employee or someone from the central office.

Research universities may offer additional resources for training in grantsmanship and for other grant expenses as well—for example, matching funds. Graduate students and faculty located in these sorts of institutions should ask their colleagues about assistance and be alert for programs and opportunities from various divisions of the school.

GRANTS AND INSTITUTIONAL STRUCTURE

Because of the institutional interest in grants and because they function as a type of contract (the grant pays for certain defined activities that the institution will be held responsible for), most institutions will designate at least one person and often entire departments to assist with and monitor grant-related activities. It may not be surprising to discover that most of these offices relate to the financial side of grants. There are several reasons for this, including the need for good stewardship (meaning that funds need to be spent per donor agreement), federal requirements, and the necessity of monitoring university contributions to grants (match or cost share).

Depending on the type and size of institution, institutional oversight may feature one, some, or all of the following offices. Understanding this will help you manage relationships with staff from each office, especially when you get different answers from each of these offices to the same grant question. The answers you should listen to depend on (a) where you work in the institution, and (b) whether the office asked has prime authority over the matter in question.

The Sponsored Projects Office

Also known as academic grants or sponsored research, the sponsored projects office is dedicated to assisting with grants developed by faculty members and often staff as well. Throughout this book, I will refer to this entity as sponsored projects, or the sponsored projects office, and to the staff as the sponsored projects staff. In the multiple structures of the university environment, the sponsored projects office exists, at minimum, to monitor the commitments the university makes to external academic funders. At the very least, sponsored projects personnel will check budgets and monitor compliance with institutional, federal, and funder regulations. At some colleges and universities the sponsored projects office is established to assist faculty in grant seeking as well. The sponsored projects office often has the last word on federal and other government submissions, the interpretation of guidelines, and relations with federal funders.

The Nuts and Bolts of Grant Writing *features a section at the end of most chapters called "Working with Your Sponsored Projects Office." These sections highlight the processes of each step of the submission that will probably most concern your sponsored projects office, whether you are working with the central office or a department staff member.*

Corporate and Foundation Relations

The corporate and foundation relations office is most often run by advancement, university relations, or development and forms their grant seeking and stewardship unit. The corporate and foundation relations office's view of grants will be based primarily on foundation giving.[1] For the most part, this point of view stems from a mission to fund core university priorities, like scholarships, endowments, buildings, and presidential initiatives. These development grant writers probably maintain the primary relationships with the foundations most interested in your institution—these are generally the foundations with campus buildings named after them. For a faculty member, working with corporate and foundation relations can be a helpful experience because they normally "own" relationships with foundations and so can introduce faculty to funding opportunities. On the other hand, corporate and foundation relations may expect some control over a project, and this may or may not benefit faculty research interests. Corporate and foundation relations often has the last word on proposals to foundations, interpretation of foundation guidelines (especially when they are not research based), and relations with foundations.

The Nuts and Bolts of Grant Writing *features a section at the end of many chapters called "Working With the Corporate and Foundation Relations Office." In this section you will find tips for working with members of the development grant writing staff as well as projections about what their concerns might be for each part of the submission process.*

---

[1] In smaller institutions, however, corporate and foundation relations or development may have some sponsored projects functions, including working with federal projects and helping with subcontracts.

Advancement

Also known as University Relations and Development, Advancement is the umbrella division for corporate and foundation relations, handling not only grants but also donations and external, government, and alumni relations. Funds are brought in by development primarily on the basis of relationships rather than grant writing: Even corporate and foundation relations grants often have a strong relationship component to them. These offices are often considered an arm of the president's office and are likely to have access to deans and vice presidents as well

Figure 2.2 An Example of Institutional Reporting Lines

President
Represents
Organization
and
Fundraises

Chief Advancement Officer
Lead Fundraiser

Chief Academic Officer/Provost
Lead Academic

Development (Donor/Gift Work)

External Relations Offices

Deans

Vice President for Research

Academic Support Services

Corporate and Foundation Relations (CFR)

Academic Depts. and Faculty

Sponsored Projects

The sponsored projects office is generally run out of academic affairs and reflects academic interests. The corporate and foundation relations office is generally run out of development and reflects fundraising interests. Accountants, the bursar, and controller generally have their own reporting lines to the president and represent the financial interests of the institution. The IRB generally falls under academic affairs.

as to the board of directors. In professional schools and extremely small institutions, all grants may be run through the development office. Development, advancement, or university relations may have the last word on donations, foundation relations, and relations with donors.

The Business Office

The business office, the controller's office, and the accounting area are common names for the fiscal side of the university or the various offices that do the books, pay the bills, and handle the finances. Even the smallest postsecondary institution will feature a business office of some type. And if the institution does not have sponsored projects, corporate and foundation relations, or a development office, the business office may assist with the budgeting and implementation of grant proposals. Collectively, any staff member who assists with implementation of a grant and especially accounting staff may be referred to as "post-award." Most academic grants require a great deal of accounting involvement, and this is especially true for federal grants. Smooth grant implementation can be strongly influenced by good relations with post-award. Post-award generally has the last word on the way institutions handle grant moneys internally and the interpretation of award stipulations, particularly those that may draw an audit or financial penalties.

The Institutional Review Board

The Institutional Review Board (IRB) is a university committee established by federal law on every university campus where human research may be conducted. The IRB's function is to consider and monitor human subjects research on campus. Any faculty member or graduate student considering the proposal of a project that involves any sort of research on human beings needs to be aware of and follow the local IRB process.

Some funders require that proof of IRB approval be included in the proposal, although others allow the PI to show that approval is pending or even to apply only if the award is made ("on award"). The tricky part of waiting to apply for IRB approval on award is that the approval process can take four to six weeks, depending on your institution. If you are allowed to apply with pending IRB approval, it is wisest to submit the application right after proposal submission in order to avoid this delay. This is also a very good time to apply because the project will be fresh in your mind. The IRB is run by faculty researchers and forms a part of academic affairs.

THE NUTS & BOLTS

1. Institutions of higher education feature unique offices to assist in grant preparation and administration, including sponsored projects, corporate and foundation relations, development, and the business office.

2. The three main types of academic grants include research grants, service grants, and fellowships.

3. Peer-reviewed competitions run in a manner similar to peer-reviewed journals: Other academics will score the proposals.

4. Styles of grant seeking may be strongly affected by the receiving institution and the field of the PI.

EXERCISES: WORKING TOWARD MASTERY

1. Institutional Information

   a. Describe the institution you are associated with, including student population, highest degree, number of commuter students, and so forth. Provide as much information as possible. The most updated information is probably located on your institution's website, in the admissions area.
   b. What is the most prominent academic feature of your institution? For example, is it strongly agricultural, business-oriented, steeped in the humanities? Does it have a particularly prominent school or department? Does your school have historical importance? While this information may be on the website, you may also need to ask colleagues or different campus offices about this. The library staff and sponsored projects may have answers to these questions.
   c. What is your position within your institution?
   d. What grant services do you have access to? If the answers are not on the Web page, you may need to talk to staff members from the sponsored projects office.

2. Find the research page on your institutional website and look over the awards made over the past three years. Record the following:

   a. How many awards were made?
   b. What funder made the most awards to your institution?
   c. How much and from which funder was the highest award over the last three years? Who was the PI?
   d. How much and from which funder was the lowest award over the last three years?

   e. What was the average award made over the last three years?

   f. Looking at these awards, which PI is doing work that is most closely related to your work?

   g. Find the sponsored projects page. Institutionally, what will be a faculty member's first few steps to submit a grant?

   h. How would you, in your current situation at your institution, go about applying for a grant?

CHAPTER TERMS

Development: The department at a college, university, or professional graduate school dedicated to raising funds through grants and gifts. Development is normally a subunit of advancement or university relations.

Indirect cost rate (overhead): This is a percentage of the direct costs of a project added on to the total request to pay for such resources as electricity, building maintenance, libraries, accounting infrastructure, and so forth, which are difficult to measure.

Institutional review board (IRB): A federally mandated postsecondary committee at all colleges and universities that reviews all research involving human subjects.

PUI (predominantly undergraduate institution): A college or university with a strong teaching mission, for example, liberal arts colleges, comprehensive universities, and community colleges.

STEM (science, technology, engineering, and mathematics): The science, technology, engineering, and mathematics disciplines at a college or university.

3

Funders

INTRODUCTION

The focus of this chapter will be funders, both government and foundation: what they are, how to build relations with them, and how to figure out whether your project is a good match to their interests. This is an important question because there are thousands of foundations and many government agencies in the United States. In fact, the Foundation Directory, the premiere foundation search service, features 108,000 foundations and nonfederal grant makers (Foundation Center, 2013). If you are marveling at this large number and thinking that somewhere among all these funders there must be a fit for your project, then you are on the right track.

Although for many faculty and staff members at universities a federal grant is the gold standard, government grants are not always where new PIs begin. Many academic researchers as well as project directors begin seeking grants from local foundations first. You can ladder your grant efforts by applying to foundations for smaller awards and then work your way up to larger federal awards. In this way, a PI builds trust through the good stewardship of small investments in her work and gradually attains the large foundation or federal awards of senior investigators.

WHAT IS A FOUNDATION?

A **foundation** is a nonprofit entity created by an individual, family, group of individuals, or corporation to distribute resources (primarily money) for specific charitable purposes. All U.S. foundations must file a **990-PF** (990) with the Internal Revenue Service (IRS) each year to account for yearly activity.

Private foundations are often created by individuals or families with wealth generated from their businesses, and/or from initial public offerings when a company becomes a corporation. Corporations can also create private foundations that operate from ongoing distributions from the parent entity. Some foundations, called *operating foundations*, only fund their own programs, meaning that they do not make external awards.

Public foundations derive their funding from a wider array of sources, including other foundations, donors, and even government agencies. In fact, some public foundations are actually quasi-governmental entities. For example, the Institute of International Education (IIE), which administers the Fulbright Programs, receives about 66 percent of its funding from U.S. government agencies (Institute of International Education, 2011). Others, like local **community foundations**, are supported mainly by individual and corporate donations.

Box 3.1   Many Types of Foundations

Foundations as a population are very diverse and are governed in many different ways. Foundation management can run the gamut from very involved founder families who are teaching their children philanthropy, to relatively impersonal corporate affairs and everything in between. When you are creating a relationship with a foundation, try to research it. Find out how it was founded and how it is governed. Get a sense of the composition of the staff because it is always better to know whether the person returning your call is an assistant, program officer, trustee, or a child of the founder!

Another area of diversity for foundations relates to staffing and organization. Larger foundations tend to have well-developed areas of interest led by program officers or directors who are area experts and very knowledgeable about the funding process. Program officers at major foundations may have doctorates and may even be former university faculty. Small foundations may have one administrative assistant or coordinator who holds down the fort while the busy chair of the board (probably a volunteer) flits in and out of the office in between running quarterly board meetings. Show patience when foundation personnel appear late in replying to an email or telephone call, because foundations are often understaffed.

EXAMPLE OF A FOUNDATION FUNDING PROCESS

The foundation board meets and board members discuss the direction they would like awards to take and how much money will be available during the next funding cycle. They create a set of parameters regarding the kinds of projects they are interested in, possibly including the types of organizations preferred, the number and size of awards, and what the **allowable costs** will be. (Allowable costs include all budget items that a funder is willing to cover as part of an award.)

Information about this opportunity is made available. The guidelines or RFP may be posted on a website, onto Facebook, emailed to potential PIs, or simply printed on a sheet of paper to be mailed out. Major programs might put together a webinar or question and answer session, and a program officer or other staff members may be available to answer questions about the opportunity.

The foundation receives proposals responding to the opportunity until the deadline.

Staff members sift through the proposals and separate out those that do not respond to the guidelines. Proposals that suggest unrelated projects as well as those that do not follow formatting instructions may be immediately returned, unread, or they may be held until the competition is over when all applicants will be informed of their status.

Proposals are sent to be reviewed, whether it is by the foundation board or by faculty peer reviewers.

Proposals are divided into two categories: declines, which receive notification; and awardees, which receive award letters, further instructions, and possibly (after some negotiation) checks.

Box 3.2 The Nuts & Bolts: What If There Is No Deadline?

Foundations do not always set deadlines for grant competitions—which means that you can often submit a proposal year round. Of course, the actual work cycle of most foundations is usually formed around board meetings, which are generally quarterly. If you prefer to plan your submissions around deadlines and want to make best use of time, then find out the dates of the board meetings for the year. Submitting a proposal a few weeks before a board meeting means that it has a better chance of consideration during the upcoming meeting, and you will avoid waiting an additional three to four months before the next opportunity for consideration.

WHAT ARE GOVERNMENT FUNDERS?

There are a large variety of state, county, and city grant opportunities available for faculty and staff to compete for. Because each of the 50 states and a multitude of counties and cities run programs differently, however, *The Nuts and Bolts* will not delve into all of these funding sources. Careful readers will be prepared to apply for state, county, and city opportunities through the materials presented in this book, because the number one rule is always the same: Follow directions. To find these sources, explore state, county, and city websites as well as professional listservs.

Federal Awards

Federal agencies are established by legislative statutes and operate with funding approved annually through congressional appropriations. There are a great many agencies and subagencies within agencies as well as a variety of awarding and contracting priorities, policies, and mechanisms within all of these. Different federal agencies award grants for a great variety of work. Some agencies are formed to develop research, like the NSF or the National Institutes of Health (NIH). For others, research is encouraged; however the agency may also be interested in applied and service projects—for example, the U.S. Department of Education, the U.S. Department of Justice, or the U.S. Department of Commerce.

Each agency has a unique organizational culture that affects how grants are offered, awarded, and implemented. If there is one agency that closely fits your project, take the time to get to know it thoroughly. Federal submissions are more complex in some ways than foundation submissions; there are simply more rules, procedures, and guidelines to be aware of. The faster you can become familiar with these the easier time you will have as you prepare your submission.

The good news is that all federal agencies follow specific grant regulations set out by the Office of Management and Budget (OMB). The OMB rules for institutions of higher education are primarily financial. The one most important document to the proposal process is the A-21, Cost Principles for Educational Institutions. We will discuss the A-21 in more detail in Chapter 6; however, for now keep in mind that the A-21 and other OMB rules help unite federal granting and give it consistency.

Federal grants are often preferred by higher education faculty and staff because of the following:

- They are more likely to be awarded over multiple years.
- They normally allow collaborations with colleagues at other institutions.

Figure 3.1   The A-21 and Federal Agencies

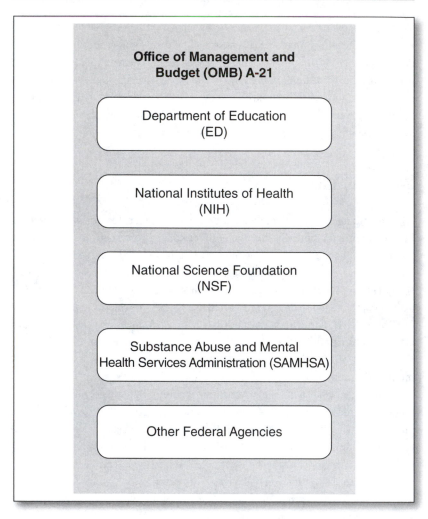

The A-21 and other OMB documents govern granting divisions of all federal agencies. These rules create similarities between the many agencies of the federal government.

- They are often comprehensive to project needs.
- They are often awarded on the basis of peer review, which means that even though the money comes from the government, the award decision was made on the basis of peer (faculty) opinion.

Requests for Proposals

Federal opportunities often take the form of requests for proposals (RFPs). Ideally, an RFP is a relatively complete set of guidelines for submission to a competition and a convenient way for an organization to offer grants in addition to other activities. An RFP will include information about the funder, award information, award terms, the goals of the competition, eligibility, and, hopefully, a rubric and guidelines. RFPs, which do not have page limits, have the tendency to cause the grant description to become very long and sometimes rambling.

FINDING A GOOD FIT

For the rest of this chapter we will consider foundation and federal opportunities together, because many of the same processes are involved in planning for foundation and federal submissions. Significant differences will be discussed as they come up.

No one ever got a grant by proposing the wrong idea to the wrong funder. A foundation with strong Dalmatian dog programs, for example, will not fund kitten shelters; they fund projects for dogs and not just any kind of dog—they fund projects for Dalmatian dogs. Similarly, medical funders are probably not going to be interested in poverty projects; political science funders will probably not want to see stem cell research; and behavioral funders really do not want to see Freudian analytical projects. When you stop to consider how many hours go into the preparation of a grant proposal, the importance of a good grant search becomes very clear. Finding an opportunity that fits the project is an important step toward a great proposal.

Funders make their interests known in several ways. Different funders, both federal and foundation, publicize their programs in different ways, so sometimes you will need to be persistent and check in more than one place to find the information you need to make a decision about a submission.

Websites are probably the most common current method used by all funders to make their guidelines available to potential PIs. A regularly updated website is the place to check for changes to guidelines, deadlines, and other important submission matters. Note that federal funders may have different programs with similar names, so check websites carefully.

Databases are also very good places to get information on foundation and federal funders. The most prominent of these for foundations is the Foundation Directory Online by the Foundation Center. Grants.gov is the primary information clearinghouse for federal grants, and there are also several academic databases that offer federal opportunities as well as research foundation opportunities, for example Pivot and SciVal.

Writing to (or calling) a foundation without a website may be necessary. There are still foundations out there that do not have websites and perhaps do not have email, although the numbers are small. The guidelines of such a foundation will normally come back to you as a letter by post.

Googling funders can be helpful to get news on them, their grantees, and their structure, directors, or trustees. This is especially useful when researching a foundation that does not have a very extensive website; however, it can be a useful practice to understand any funder better.

990s can be consulted to ascertain a foundation's board of directors, grants for a specific year, and contact information.

Facebook and Twitter now feature information from some major funders.

Project Intent Versus Funder Guidelines

Knowing exactly what you want to do in your project can strongly affect which funder(s) you ultimately choose to approach. On the other hand, having a less defined project can help you mold it to funder guidelines, which may help you get funded. Throughout your career, you will probably approach grant searches at different times in both states of mind, sometimes knowing exactly what you want to do, other times not as sure.

We will be discussing the various aspects of how to interpret funder information and make decisions about whether a project fits or whether it needs to change throughout this chapter. For now, please keep the following in mind:

- Proposing a project that does not fit funder guidelines is a waste of your time (and your time is valuable, of course).
- The guidelines are generally firm. The project must be fit to them, not vice versa.
- The best information on fit may be found in previously funded grants (more on this later).

Allowable Costs

In addition to funder program interests, there is also the very important consideration of allowable costs or what sorts of things the funder will allow an award to be spent on. Of course, you are not expected to have a full budget at this early point; however, it is a good idea to have a sense of what sorts of costs you will request, because this can affect the funder you choose. In addition, it is also very helpful to have a sense of the scale of what you are proposing. Obviously a potential award of $25,000 will create a very different project than $100,000 or $1,000,000.

While federal grants famously have a standard list of unallowable costs (covered in Chapter 6), foundations present real diversity on this question. Some will fund whatever you need, and others have restrictions, sometimes many restrictions. One important restriction that graduate students and adjunct faculty need to be aware of is that some funders will only fund faculty PIs or PhD holders with a permanent full-time job at a university (although not necessarily tenure). Of course, many graduate students can team up with their advisors to submit such a grant; however, it is very important to know when this is the case and plan accordingly from the beginning of the submission process.

Some foundations specialize in capital projects, which are the creation and renovation of buildings. Others refuse to pay salaries or perhaps fringe benefits, and many will not pay indirect costs or the costs of running a project (for example, the cost of rent, building maintenance, electricity, accounting services, etc.). Federal funders famously will refuse to pay for celebrations, food, or anything that is not directly related to work.

Putting Intent and Allowable Costs Together

When considering applying to a funder, a balance must be struck between what the funder intends to accomplish with the program (program goals or intent), allowable costs, and what your project requires to run properly.

As I have attempted to express with Figure 3.2 your proposal needs to match the intent of the funder and request only allowable costs. It is possible that there will be aspects of your project that are not included in the proposal because they do not fit with the program intent or they represent unallowable costs. The question will be whether enough of your project fits into the proposal (meaning it matches the guidelines and allowable costs) to make an application to this funder worth the effort involved.

Figure 3.2   Triple Chart

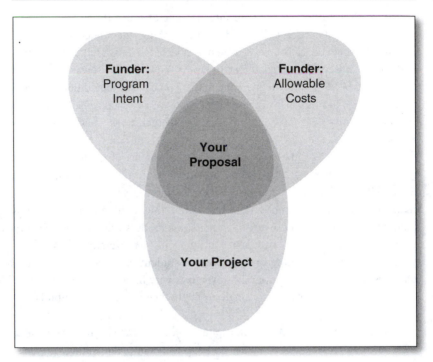

This chart demonstrates how the proposal is created at the conjunction of the program intent, the allowable costs, and the project.

The smart PI will have a preliminary answer to all of these questions answered before searching:

- What is my project all about? What will it accomplish?
- What sorts of things must be paid for?
- About how much will the total project cost?

Box 3.3 The Nuts & Bolts:
Complexity in Project Fit

One way to think about the relationship between program intent, allowable costs, and the project would be to jot aspects of the project down on the triple chart, as I have (Figure 3.3). In the circular central area (Your Proposal) I only included aspects of the project that reflect program intent and allowable costs. In the lower

Figure 3.3   Triple Chart With a Project

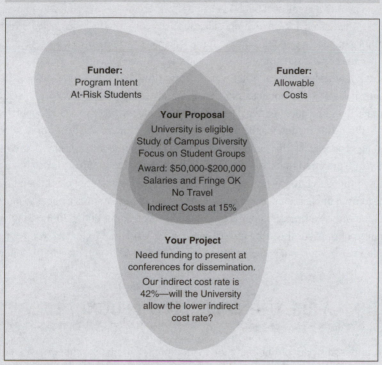

Funder:
Program Intent
At-Risk Students

Funder:
Allowable
Costs

Your Proposal

University is eligible
Study of Campus Diversity
Focus on Student Groups

Award: $50,000-$200,000
Salaries and Fringe OK
No Travel

Indirect Costs at 15%

Your Project

Need funding to present at
conferences for dissemination.

Our indirect cost rate is
42%—will the University
allow the lower indirect
cost rate?

central area under the Your Proposal section, I jotted down aspects of the project that do not match funder intent and allowable costs.

Here we see that two aspects of the project are not covered by the funder: funding for travel and part of the indirect cost rate. Both of the uncovered aspects of the project are probably minor: Presentation funding is not going to make or break the project and can probably be sought elsewhere. Similarly, most universities will approve a smaller indirect cost rate when it is foundation policy. Such a project, therefore, could probably move forward, depending on institution policy.

If there were too many funding items left out of the central proposal area of this illustration, yet the guidelines were extremely close to the intent of the project, then we would need to make a choice between the following:

- Not proposing the project
- Proposing part of the project and running an incomplete project
- Proposing part of the project and obtaining the remaining resources elsewhere (like other funders)

Multiple Funders

There is a great deal of competition out there for grants, and this manifests in declines, even for good proposals. Similarly, one of the open secrets of the grants game is that people who get funded also get turned down a great deal. This is because the more proposals you submit the more chances you have to be awarded and declined. In other words, submitting a well-written proposal many times increases the chances that it will be awarded. Along the way, this same proposal will be declined too. Developing patience for this process is important.

What this means for the beginning PI is that he may need to submit several strong proposals to the same funder or to various funders to get one award. It is therefore preferred to have several funders to propose to at any one time and to get those proposals into the funders' hands right away. This is somewhat different from the journal publications process, of course, where the PI submits a paper to journal editors one at a time. It is perfectly fine and even recommended to have multiple grant proposals for the same project pending with different funders. If you get multiple awards, your sponsored projects office will help you negotiate with the funders.

BUILDING A RELATIONSHIP WITH A FOUNDATION

An important part of obtaining (or maintaining) foundation support is building good relationships with foundation staff. In fact, when a foundation knows you and values your work, it is possible that they will call on you to work on a specific project. This is an extremely high compliment and only comes with integrity, hard work, focus on a similar mission, and friendly, professional contact with the foundation.

Relationships do not necessarily begin with an award, however. They effectively begin with the first contact you have with a foundation. This means the first time you call to clarify the guidelines or to ask why you were declined, you are working on the relationship. Comport yourself with this view in mind. Demonstrate professional communication and conduct. Be knowledgeable of and sensitive to staff members' concerns.

It may be appropriate for you to call the foundation to pursue questions you may have. This is a good thing to do; however, there are several points to consider:

- Check to be sure your question has not already been answered in foundation materials.
- Check for instructions on how to contact the foundation and follow these.
  a. Foundations without a telephone number listed may not want to be contacted.

    b. Foundations without email listed may not use email for business communication. An old-fashioned letter, sent by post, may be required.

- The foundation may be understaffed and busy, so be patient.

It is important to keep in mind that your institution's corporate and foundation relations office may work hard to regulate contact between foundation staff and university personnel. In spite of this, my experience has been that foundation program officers like to talk directly to PIs and that good relationships can be formed in this way. It is probably a good rule of thumb to discuss your project with foundation staff if you get the opportunity; however, when financial decisions need to be made, call in appropriate university personnel (whether that is the sponsored projects office or corporate and foundation relations). Business matters need to be run in conjunction with the institution, even when you have formed the relationship, because ultimately, the institution will be held legally responsible for the grant and the work.

WORKING WITH YOUR SPONSORED PROJECTS OFFICE

At most institutions, the sponsored projects office is established to assist and monitor faculty and staff members pursuing research grants. Some sponsored projects operations are completely centralized, and others have local department-level staff members. In either case, any faculty PI should check in with the sponsored projects personnel when submitting any grant proposal. At some research universities, a graduate student may be required to work with sponsored projects as well.

Sponsored projects at MA institutions and liberal arts colleges often offer varied services, combining the purview of department-level grants personnel with the duties of the central office. Members of sponsored projects may be people with experience in federal and foundation grants and may be hired to provide hands-on assistance with grant preparation as well as compliance to university and funder regulations.

Most sponsored projects personnel do not write grants, although some may edit the narrative, and almost all of them provide budget assistance (even if that consists of letting the PI know what needs fixing in the budget!). Sponsored projects personnel will often know about grant opportunities and may distribute these to faculty. They may provide assistance in getting institutional approval of a project, and they may also submit applications to funders on behalf of the PI. First-time PIs should take the time to explore the services of the sponsored projects office and see what assistance might be available.

The sponsored projects office will often maintain Web pages on the university website, and this is a good first place to being exploration. Call or email per the contact information given, and ask questions. Make an appointment and go meet with one of the staff to discuss your project.

You may be able to expect the following from sponsored projects:

- Budget information and possibly assistance with drafting a proposal budget
- Assistance with interpreting funder guidelines
- Assistance in establishing subcontracts
- Assistance in creating and documenting partnerships across institution departments
- Possible editing assistance
- Required university forms
- Information on funding opportunities

What generally NOT to expect from your sponsored projects office includes the following:

- Grant writing services (although they may know grant writers for hire)
- Sponsored project personnel may be restricted from working with visiting, term, and part-time faculty, or graduate students.

Graduate students and nontenureline faculty should ask about the sponsored projects services available to them. If sponsored projects personnel cannot assist you directly, consider teaming up with a tenureline faculty member to realize a project.

WORKING WITH THE CORPORATE AND FOUNDATION RELATIONS OFFICE

Development grant writing staff will probably be most interested in projects that raise the profile of the institution in a very public way or bring other kinds of direct, obvious benefit to the core university functions. They tend to work on campaigns, fund buildings, raise money for scholarships, and buttress central university programs. For PIs involved in related projects, it might be worth the effort to contact corporate and foundation relations. This contact would most likely be made through the dean's office, possibly requiring the dean's permission.

In smaller institutions and professional schools, corporate and foundation relations, university relations, advancement, or development[1] may handle foundation proposals, even when faculty members apply. The thing to keep in mind when working with advancement, development, or university relations is that they often (although not always) have very limited experience with research grants.

THE NUTS & BOLTS

1. Two main considerations of funders are their mission or what they want to accomplish in the world and what types of organizations and activities they will fund, meaning how they want to accomplish the mission.

2. A foundation is a type of nonprofit philanthropic entity dedicated to funding specific types of activities, possibly including research.

3. An RFP or request for proposal is one important way for federal agencies to announce funding opportunities. Foundations often post guidelines on a website.

4. Unlike with journal publications, it is permissible, even encouraged, to send your project to multiple funders.

EXERCISES: WORKING TOWARD MASTERY

1. Close your eyes and pretend to be a participant in your project six months after it is funded. Arrive to the project: Where is it? What sort of building are you walking into? What do you see as you look around? Who do you talk to? What do they tell you? What happens next? Jot down the entire process you visualize. Now read it and pay attention. Whatever parts of this project that do not exist must be created, and what must be created needs to relate closely to the funder's interests and mission.

2. Close your eyes again. Now pretend to be the project director six months after the project has been funded. Where is your workspace? What are you doing as you arrive to it? Are there a computer and telephone there? Who are you talking to? What sorts of messages are you receiving from colleagues? What is it that you must do today? Jot down all of this and note the items that need to be funded. Would you need employee salary, rent, or money to purchase

---

[1]Although each of these designations is conceptualized differently by development staff members at various institutions, for faculty purposes, they can basically be considered the same type of office.

equipment? Sort these into the following lines: personnel, travel and hospitality, collaborators and consultants, vendor services, and miscellaneous items. As you look for funders, note which ones fund these sorts of expenses.

3. Now, based on Number 1 and 2, consider the scale of the project and its budget. Will it be a one-person operation, so perhaps under $100,000? Is it a large multipartner collaboration, perhaps closer to $1 million?

CHAPTER TERMS

990-PF (990): A form that nonprofits must file annually with the U.S. Internal Revenue Service (IRS) that summarizes financial activities for the year. This document includes grant awards paid out, approach and contact information, and a list of the board of directors, in addition to other useful information.

Allowable costs: The categories of budget items that a funder will allow a grant to pay for. This is a formal term in federal grants that have a specific list of allowable costs (see Chapter 6); however, this book uses the term to refer to foundation cost preferences as well.

Community foundation: A foundation that manages the contributions of many separate donors and provides the services necessary to distribute or award these funds to benefit the residents of a defined geographic area.

Foundation: A legal entity created by an individual, family, group of individuals, or corporation to distribute money for specific charitable purposes.

4

Searching

INTRODUCTION

Half the battle of grant seeking is finding the right opportunity: Having a project that fits neatly into a funder's guidelines is a sweet spot. It is not always easy to get to that sweet spot, however: Locating opportunities and sifting through them can be a time-consuming process. It is worth the effort because projects that fit funder guidelines are more likely to win awards.

This chapter will cover the process of searching in some detail for both foundation and federal funders. We will discuss foundation and research databases as well as Grants.gov, the federal grants clearinghouse. The mechanics of searching are essentially the same for federal and foundation records, although you will probably notice some difference in the materials. Foundations tend to produce more streamlined information, while federal grant information can stretch over a large number of pages.

WHERE TO FIND GRANTS

Grant opportunity information can be found in many places. Potential funders can be located through word of mouth, listservs, and newsletters; however, two of the most efficient ways to look for grants are through disciplinary organizations, like the American Political Science Association (APSA), the American Educational Research Association (AERA), the American Psychological Association (APA), and so forth, and through grants databases. We will cover both sources here.

Professional Organizations

Many disciplinary organizations either offer grant opportunities directly to members or feature information on funders of interest on the organization website. For example, the APA has a really excellent set of opportunities available on the main website (www.apa.org), under "Research." Disciplinary funding programs will comprise some of the strongest leads for research grants because, although they often award small amounts, they may be more likely to award bench or exploratory research. Disciplinary organizations normally peer-review submissions, and this brings increased prestige to associated grant awards.

Scholarly organizations often offer funding opportunities just for graduate students and specifically for dissertation research. There are also often career-starter grants for junior faculty, so make sure to check the relevant websites for your disciplinary organizations early and often.

Box 4.1 Making Connections: Finding Grants

Where else can you find grant opportunities? Consider chatting with the following people about grants:

- Your advisor
- Faculty and graduate student colleagues who already have grants
- A conference speaker who has landed awards
- Friendly faculty in other departments who have been awarded
- Local sponsored projects staff members

Grant Opportunity Databases

One of the most efficient ways to access grant opportunities is to begin an organized search using a grant opportunity database. University research grant databases are different from foundation grant databases in several key ways. University research grant databases (like Pivot or SciVal Funding) are subscribed to by the university and offered for free to faculty, staff, and perhaps graduate students. In addition, the following are true about university research grant databases:

- They will more than likely include both major foundations and federal opportunities.
- They will tend to be heavy on research opportunities and lighter on direct service opportunities.
- They will probably emphasize STEM (science, technology, engineering, and mathematics) grants.

Social science and service grant opportunities are included in these databases; however, one must learn to use filters to pare back the many STEM opportunities that will probably appear also.

In addition, there are foundation databases (like the Foundation Directory Online or Guidestar) that may be available through sponsored projects or corporate and foundation relations. Individuals can subscribe to both of these databases if they are not available on campus. Foundation databases (a) include foundations rather than federal grant opportunities, (b) will feature many nonresearch funders, and (c) will have many service opportunities.

If you do not have access to a grant-searching database through your institution, there are still options.

Many large cities offer access to grant databases through public libraries, so visit a local library website, or call and ask.

There are local foundation libraries scattered around the United States that will normally offer free access to databases. The Foundation Center maintains a list of cooperating foundation libraries on its website. Be sure to check online or call ahead, as these facilities may offer limited hours for public access.

Elite university libraries may offer access to funding databases, and they may allow community members to access their databases while on premises. Check the relevant website, or call and ask.

Use a free database: Guidestar, itself a nonprofit, maintains a database of U.S. nonprofits and foundations. Anyone can run a free basic search after online registration. Although only a few fields are easily accessible with this option, one does get the organization's 990, which includes the most useful bits of information, as we will discuss later.

Googling funders can bring helpful results, and one can find free online grant opportunity databases that emphasize various political points of view. If you run this sort of search, it is wise to check your results against the basic (free) Guidestar information on any particular funder.

Once access to a database is established, it will be helpful to undertake any training that is made available. Having facility with your database will save time in the long run.

DATABASE SEARCH TECHNIQUES

Most of the usual rules of database searching apply when using grant opportunity databases. Remember that the more words you use to define your topic, the more likely that you are making the topic very specific, and this can lead to fewer opportunities. In this case, begin shortening your search term list. On the other hand, the fewer words you use, generally, the more broad the search. If you come up with hundreds or thousands of opportunities, begin adding terms to make your search more specific.

There are some differences between foundation grant opportunity databases and university grant opportunity databases that should be kept in mind.

University Research Grant Opportunity Databases

Most university research databases are heavy on STEM opportunities, and this can make finding social science and humanities competitions somewhat more difficult. There are a few tricks, however, that can help you locate useful grants.

Define your project against STEM opportunities. STEM opportunities are dominant in university research databases. To figure out the proper filter, run the basic search and then check to see what kinds of opportunities come up. Build a filter that will deflect the specific STEM opportunities that you do not want. For example, a social scientist researching the behavioral or social effects of alcoholism may run into a great deal of literature regarding its medical aspects, so a useful search with filter might be

FIND Alcoholism NOT Medical.

You may need to build the filter out quite a bit as you go along. Think of setting the filters as an iterative process.

Check out the standardized database filters, or exclude options. Here are a few common ones:

- **Geography:** Americans should remove non-U.S. opportunities. After all, will the Mongolian government really fund U.S. history in Cincinnati?
- **Funding instrument:** Be aware of the types of funding instruments available. Besides the standard grant instrument, some social scientists (like criminologists, educators, psychologists, or medical sociologists) may be able to set up cooperative agreements or contracts to provide services and do some research as well.

- **PI eligibility:** Be aware of how status affects awards. While there are fellowships created especially for graduate students, many awards are directed toward tenured faculty.
- **Do NOT filter according to deadline:** Many federal competitions are held regularly, and while you may have missed a recent deadline there may be upcoming competitions in the next few months or the next year.

Search broadly. Try not to define the search too narrowly. In many cases, social science opportunities are less specific, and so you will need more abstract terms. For example, an anthropologist interested in African kin groups might find the best chance for funding in a general anthropology or general social science opportunity.

Interdisciplinary. Try searching based on a related discipline if the topic is in any way potentially interdisciplinary.

PI publications. Some of the databases will allow searches on the basis of publications. While the beginning PI may not have very many at this stage, he may be able to use the template of a more senior faculty member doing similar work to search for opportunities.

Talk to the database company. Each database is different and has its own idiosyncrasies. Talking to a company representative may help you figure out the best ways to search according to the specific system as well as additional filters that may provide real help. Remember, the company wants your university to use the database, so they will normally be very helpful in answering questions and providing training to you as an authorized university user.

Box 4.2 True Story

If you are like me, when you begin working with a database you would probably skip looking at the categories or keyword list and just jump into searching. I learned the hard way, though, that the keyword list, the company's concept of the topics covered in the database, is a very important resource.

How did I learn this? It was way back during my first grant writing job for a mental health center. Part of my assignment was to find new opportunities to pursue, and of course, that is how I became acquainted with the Foundation Directory Online.

As I was playing with the search mechanism, I noticed that searches for crisis services and eating disorders did not show results; however, I eventually discovered

(Continued)

(Continued)

that both of these terms came under "mental health," not under "crisis services" or "eating disorders." The term "teenager" did not appear at all, although the terms "adolescent," "youth," "young adult," and "transition age youth" (TAY) did.

Figuring this out was helpful, because although I could (and do) run searches using a text search of whatever word I want, it is always good to be thorough and check for items under the database's own organizational system. I recommend that you trawl through the program areas, fields of interest, or keywords and get a sense of how things are categorized and what the database nomenclature is for the kind of project you are interested in. Use these words in searching in addition to terms from the academic literature and any others that you might think of to run more effective searches.

Foundation Grant Opportunity Databases

Remember that foundations primarily fund service projects and charitable activity. Foundation databases therefore are created for fundraisers, and so their program descriptions will be tailored to laymen and not researchers. Consider how a journalist or schoolteacher might describe your project, and use some of those words in your search.

Get to know the indexing categories. Take some time to explore the database indexing categories for project and organization activities. This will give you an idea of where your project falls within the database nomenclature.

Pay attention to geography. Foundations may fund locally, they may fund specific nonlocal projects, or they may fund nationally or internationally. Some databases allow you to search on the basis of the location of grants made, which is wiser than searching on the basis of funder location:

- **Some foundations fund exclusively elsewhere.** There are foundations located in one place but established to assist people of another area. Be alert for this.
- **Foundations often reflect local geographic patterns**. Consider how people think about your region or area—if the pattern is strong enough, you may see it in foundation-award patterns. For example, there are very few foundations in California that fund the entire state (with the exception of the Irvine Foundation). San Francisco foundations tend to fund Northern

California, and Los Angeles foundations tend to fund Southern California. This becomes problematic because you cannot easily filter by city in most foundation databases.

Accepting or not accepting proposals. Be aware that some foundations in the database may not accept unsolicited proposals. This certainly can present a challenge; however, it may not be insurmountable:

- **Is this an error?** I have found that sometimes foundations are erroneously marked as not accepting unsolicited proposals. It might be worth your effort to check the 990 to be sure that this information is correct.
- **Pursue this foundation anyway.** If your project matches the guidelines very closely and the foundation is active, it may be possible to bring your project to the attention of foundation personnel through letters, telephone calls, and so forth. Your institution's corporate and foundation relations office could be very helpful in such an endeavor.

Large and small awards. You may be able to filter out small awards or foundations that do not make many awards, or you may be able to filter out extremely large awards. Depending on your experience level and the position you hold, small awards may be a waste of time and large awards may be out of reach (for now).

EVALUATING DATABASE RECORDS

No one looks forward to sifting through 100 or more records, searching for a handful of appropriate funders. Even so, this is an important step to undertake if you want to make a database search work. The good news is that most databases have broken record information into handy fields, and this makes a relatively quick perusal possible. Most database records will generally give identifying information (name, address, and contact information) first, then mission, amount of funding available, limitations or eligibility, programs, and past grants in some sort of order. The past grants section often comes last.

The key to an efficient search is to look at eligibility or limitations first.

Limitations and/or Eligibility

While the standard searching advice is to have a look at every record in the search results, it is not

> **True Story**
>
> *The best advice I ever got for submitting a successful proposal was simple: "Follow directions."*

necessary to read each record completely. The time for the thorough consideration of a record will come when you are honing in on what looks like a good fit.

When dealing with long lists of results, the first timesaving suggestion is to read eligibility and limitations first, NOT the mission of the funder or program description. There is no point to reading the various sections of an opportunity if for some reason your project will not qualify. So, not only should the eligibility and limitations be read first, but they should also be read doubtfully. Read them *looking* for reasons your project will not qualify.

The need for efficiency demands doubt when you are engaged in examining large numbers of records. This means looking in the text for the reasons why a particular funder will not be interested in your project. It means looking for the disqualification, how the project does not meet the funder's requirements, or how the funding mechanism will not work. When such a reason is found, the smart PI stops reading and gets to the next record in the search results. This saves time and cuts through some potentially misleading aspects of a funder's presentation as well.

The mission of the foundation or the purpose of the funding program is usually full of hope, promise, and positive, uplifting language. These sections also tend to be vague for the purposes of a grant seeker. For example, consider the following mission statement:

> *The Tree Project was established by the Brian family with the purpose of planting, protecting, and understanding trees and the urban forest in particular. We believe that every tree is important in and of itself, as well as providing assistance to human beings and animals, in the form of helping in the fight against global climate change, and providing shade and beauty. The Tree Project seeks to fund activities in line with its mission. For more information, please see our guidelines.*

This message of hope does not tell me how the Tree Project awards grants. If I read this mission on behalf of my local university urban forest initiative, my imaginative mind might race with the possibilities—funds to plant more trees! We could extend our seedling area! Protection! We could do more maintenance for our current plantings! Oh, and understanding! We could do some research on our unique forestry techniques! I could get very excited about this opportunity.

Only when I read the eligibility and guidelines will I know how the board of the Tree Project means to make this mission actually happen.

> *Eligibility*
>
> *The Tree Project funds grassroots nonprofit organizations. Proof of 501 (c)3 status is required.*
>
> *Limitations*
>
> *The Tree Project does not fund national organizations or universities. The Tree Project does not offer funds for the following activities:*
>
> ✓ *Purchasing seedlings*
> ✓ *Administrative costs (including indirect costs)*
> ✓ *Research*
> ✓ *Travel*
> ✓ *Charitable or political donations*

According to these guidelines, there is no funding for universities, and so the PI situated at a university should stop reading at the first line of limitations and go to the next record. Because the university PI did not read the mission, examination of this record may have taken the few seconds needed to begin reading the limitations. In this way, you can completely avoid considering the mission of a funder that will not fund your project.

The Funder's Mission

After reading through all sections on eligibility for a particular grant maker and finding no limitations or rules that would disqualify the project, then it is time to read the mission or the program description. Your doubtful stance can be relaxed somewhat, although this is the time to be very honest. Do the goals of your project match the intent of the funder?

When a funding program is set up, the people behind it generally have definite aims that they would like to accomplish in the world, whether that is funding Catholic religious orders or the search for a cure for cancer. The funder took the care to write up a mission statement or project description to communicate their intent to potential PIs. So, as you read the description or mission statement, ask yourself how your project would help accomplish the stated goals of the funder. Try to evaluate the fit from the funder's point of view, because in the long run, that is how your project will be assessed if it is submitted.

As you attempt to consider the project from the funder's point of view, note the parts that could be changed to something the funder might find more amenable. Perhaps the funder might prefer an intervention taking place as part of an

Figure 4.1   Flow Chart for Evaluation of Database Records

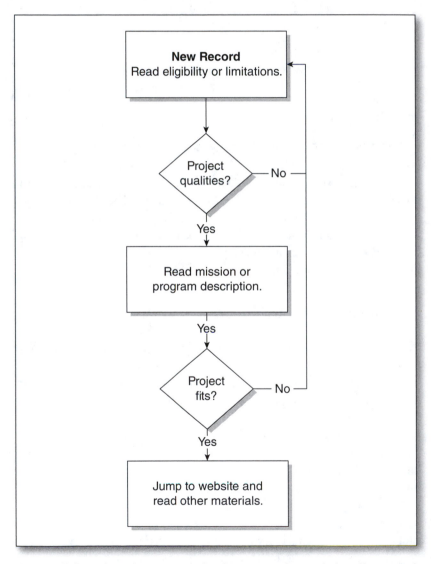

This small flow chart demonstrates the decisions to be made for efficient and quick evaluation of database records.

afterschool program rather than as part of the school day. Perhaps the funder would be interested in the research as long as the final report addressed public policy for the entire state rather than the county. Are these changes you would be willing to make? If they are not or if the mission just does not match your project goals, go on to the next record. If the mission matches your project well or you are willing to make some changes, keep reading until you have read all of the record—you are still combing for potential challenges, after all. If the record seems like a good fit, then either mark it in the database or jot down the name and go back to sifting through records.

Past Grants Search and Mining the 990

The final check for a good opportunity is a past grants search. Looking at what has already been funded may tell you a great deal about whether a funder might be interested in your project. Moreover, looking at past grants will also give you a sense of whether the funder really awards in your geographical area—unfortunately some foundations list various states and cities of funding interest but do not actually award in these areas very often.

Although it is true that past grants do not guarantee future results, it is also true that foundations tend to form funding habits. Evidence of funding in your area for similar types of organizations and/or projects is encouraging and should increase your resolve to approach a funder. Past grants can be found in a few different places:

A good grant opportunity database will feature a section of grants awarded. It is important for the PI to keep in mind that she is probably getting a selection of the grants awarded, however, not all of them. The more complete the list, the better.

Many foundations feature successful projects on their websites. This may be just a selection of grants awarded or it may be a complete list.

Federal agencies often maintain searchable lists of funded grants on their websites. If an agency does not, you might be able to put a list together on the basis of press releases, which will be in a different part of the agency website.

Foundations are required to file a 990, a report on foundation activities, with the IRS each year. In it the foundation must describe its mission and how it distributed grants over that particular fiscal year. This list will generally be the most complete one you will find for a foundation.

The 990, therefore, is where the whole story is. Databases get information from the 990, and sometimes the information that appears there is very different from what appears on a foundation website. It is always good to check the 990 of a foundation under consideration for a proposal.

Many grant opportunity databases make 990s available for download; however, if you do not have access, check Guidestar. Guidestar makes 990s available as PDFs for free once you sign up for their basic account.

Box 4.3 The Nuts & Bolts: Details on Searching the 990

The initial area to check is "Part XV Supplementary Information, 3 Grants and Contributions Paid During the Year or Approved for Future Payment," which is generally on Page 11. To make things a little more complex, many major funders will write "See Statement Attached" on Page 11 and append a list of grants paid as an appendix to the form. This is usually one of the last documents, so often the first thing I do with a 990 is to skip to the end and check for grants paid out. If the list is not at the end, it is stuck in as an attachment somewhere in the middle of the document.

Once the list of grant awards is in hand, check it for the following:

- **Similar projects.**
- **Similar organizations**. It is worth noting that some foundations tend to support a specific group of universities year in and year out. In this case, the university the PI is affiliated with must be included in the list in order to hope for consideration.
- **Projects in the PI's city or area**. The guidelines may say they fund in Vermont, for example; however, it would be best to double check and be sure that there are some actual awards that have been made to Vermont institutions, especially if the funder is located elsewhere. It is not uncommon for the guidelines to claim to fund a certain area, yet have no awards there.

GRANTS.GOV

Grants.gov is a federal clearinghouse for grant opportunities and a grant submission portal. As of 2014, Grants.gov provided access to 26 federal agencies by including information on their grant opportunities and/or functioned as a portal to accept grant submissions on their behalf. Please note that not every federal agency participates in Grants.gov, and some have dual programs through Grants.gov and through their own submission systems. If there is a specific agency that you are interested in, be sure to check its policies and procedures thoroughly so that you do not miss any opportunities and you submit correctly.

Searching Grants.gov

Searching for federal opportunities using Grants.gov is relatively straightforward; however, you may need to navigate through many screens to get to the information you are looking for. Be patient and keep clicking. Helpful points to keep in mind when searching Grants.gov include the following.

Search closed and archived opportunities. These will give you a sense of upcoming competitions, since many federal programs are annual or biannual.

Run broad keyword searches. Even if you are interested in a specific agency, it is a good idea to run the occasional keyword search across agencies. A keyword search can provide an increase in potential funders because the federal government has many overlapping areas, and multiple agencies may be interested in the same topic.

Use the eligibility filter to receive more specific opportunities, especially those tailored to public versus private colleges and universities. If you are interested in fellowships, include "individuals" in the filter because fellowships are often awarded directly to the PI. If you are collaborating with a nonprofit or other type of organization, include your partner's organization type as this may bring in more opportunities.

Searching by agency can be problematic unless you are positive you know the location of divisions or departments you are interested in. This is because what we think of as agencies may actually be part of larger divisions of the federal government and therefore may not show up in an agency search. For example, the NIH is a subagency of the Department of Health and Human Services (DHHS) and the National Institutes of Justice (NIJ) is a part of the Department of Justice (DOJ), and so forth.

Be aware of deadlines. The average federal grant requires a minimum of six weeks to properly prepare, unless you are performing a resubmission. Many people begin preparing their proposals several months ahead. Two weeks is really not enough time to create a competitive application, particularly when you take into account the submission procedures of your own university, which will probably add days or even weeks to the preparation period.

Box 4.2 True Story

I once assisted with a submission to the National Endowment for the Humanities (NEH) that had a modification two weeks before submission. This modification stated that the submission of the proposals, which is normally accomplished through Grants.gov, would instead be through an obscure portal located on the agency website. Submissions would also need a different set of forms than we usually used on Grants.gov.

We did not have much time to make the needed changes, but we succeeded in making the submission on time in the new agency portal. If I had not signed up for the email updates on Grants.gov, we would have submitted incorrectly and the proposal would have been disqualified.

Moral of the story: Always sign up for email updates when you are interested in an opportunity on Grants.gov!

Once you have applied to a particular agency a few times, its ways of organizing opportunities will become familiar. For example, people who work with the Department of Education, the NSF, and the NIH know that application information is to be found on their websites directly, not necessarily on Grants.gov. Yet the Grants.gov search is still useful because through it one can discover new agencies that might be interested in funding the project. One can also make comparisons between opportunities relatively easily. In fact, PIs interested in the NIH may find it easier to search for NIH opportunities through Grants.gov than using the NIH website, which tends to be a bit enigmatic. On the other hand PIs interested in the NSF should stick to the NSF website, which is very self-contained and has its own independent submission portal (FastLane).

Reading a Federal RFP

Federal RFPs tend to run in the direction of completeness rather than clarity or ease of use, and this can translate into tens, even hundreds, of pages of policy language. The use of templates by the agencies to relay basic information can also be a problem, especially when templates that need to be updated are included automatically, without consideration of how relevant they are or whether they are repetitive. A federal opportunity can also be a passage from the legislation that produced it or a page from the Federal Register. Be ready for a variety of documents organized in a variety of ways.

It is important to read the RFP negatively just as one would read a record from a funding database. The key difference here is that records from the same database are organized the same way, yet RFPs come in a wide range of organizational schemes—so assessing federal opportunities is a more complex exercise. Look first for things that might prevent your college or university from participating or the project from qualifying for support. If present, the RFP section on eligibility is generally more detailed and may offer additional information from what you may have read on the Grants.gov record. Read it looking for reasons the opportunity will not work for your project. Here are a few more tips for assessing federal RFPs.

Read the entire document before you decide to pursue any opportunity. Unpleasant surprises, such as requirements you cannot comply with, can appear anywhere in the RFP. I have seen grant requirements appear rather abruptly in the middle of unrelated paragraphs, so you must read everything to be sure the opportunity is worth the effort it will take to prepare a proposal.

Important information might not appear in the RFP, such as instructions on how to prepare a budget for the application. However, it would be a mistake to assume that on the basis of missing information there are no guidelines. There may be other documents available in other places that have further instructions for submission. The best place to begin searching for these is on the agency website.

Find out whether matching funds (cost share) are required before you decide to pursue an opportunity. Matching funds include resources the applicant institution must contribute toward the project. Do not be fooled by wording that makes a matching requirement seem optional, like "cost sharing is recommended." This kind of wording most often means that the match is required to compete effectively. Match requirements should be discussed up front and clearly with chairs, deans, the SPO, or whatever part of the university handles such considerations. Acquiring matching funds can be onerous, and this fact is a common reason for smaller institutions to decide not to pursue a competition.

Read a printout of the RFP and mark up the text. Jot down questions, notes, concerns, and so forth. This way you can more easily compare sections that seem to contradict each other, and you can prepare questions for the program officer or discussion points for your team.

Be alert for other instructions. If the RFP includes a reference to another document, acquire that document and read it as well before you decide to pursue the opportunity.

WHAT IF I CAN'T FIND ANY OPPORTUNITIES?

This happens. Appropriate opportunities can be hard to find for many reasons: Perhaps the idea is very cutting edge; perhaps the area is not popular or has gone unrecognized so far. What agency and foundation personnel recognize as social good (and therefore a funding area) may consist of generally agreed-upon topics like children's issues, homelessness, hunger, or disaster relief. This means that if you are proposing a cutting-edge topic, finding a funder may take a little more effort.

So, assuming that a project is basically fundable but search results are slim or zero, what can be done?

Troubleshooting the Search

Lack of search results often occurs because of the narrowness of search terms. Perhaps you could reframe your topic at a higher level of abstraction. For example, rather than looking for at-risk infant mental health, you might try "early childhood," "children," "mental health," and so forth. A similar idea is to break your terms up. If the topic is Indian microloans to female small business owners, you might try "India," "microloans," "international," "women," "small business," and so forth.

Are the available search terms exhausted? Have the database key terms been considered? Are there other ways to think of or describe the project? Discussing the project with an advisor, member of the team, colleague, or friend, whether they are experts or not, can help highlight more and different ways to describe or think about a project, potentially leading to new ways to frame the search and, possibly, to more results.

Reverse Search

Another way to search for funding when the project is uncommon would be to run a reverse search. Some databases do this automatically; with others you may need to be a little creative. To run this search, employ basically the same terms used in the funder search and search for nonprofits instead. The key is to find similar organizations or projects doing similar things and check their funding sources because you may find success with the same funders. Another option is to look for the ways a similar organization described the topic—perhaps terms are used that you did not think about. For a truly unusual project, the other organization can even be contacted, and you might ask the staff about how proposals have been framed. As long as you are not competing with this other organization for a source of funding (and sometimes, even if you are), you can get good advice. Such a conversation would be well worth the effort.

For research projects, check journal articles on similar topics for their funding sources. Grant teams are usually required to acknowledge their funders in publications. In this way you may find some good leads.

SHOULD I CHANGE MY PROJECT?

If you really cannot find a funder, you may be compelled to change your project idea. This is fairly easy for a research project, because in research the PI only needs to consider the balance that must be struck between pursuing the dream project and getting good work funded. PIs with high funding rates often pursue a variety of projects and may create new ones on receipt of novel guidelines—within the PI's scope of competence, of course. A PI working in his own research area at the average university will have the freedom to propose a variety of projects, taking care only to be sure that his efforts drive his career forward.

It is a much riskier proposition to change ideas for a running service project or for a nonprofit organization, including independent graduate schools. Changing a project to match funder expectations becomes problematic when the change would make an important aspect of a project impossible or when it would cause a significant diversion from a nonprofit organization's business plan or mission.

While it might be appropriate to alter the business plan from time to time to maintain pace with the environment, such decisions must always be taken carefully and thoughtfully. If changes come too quickly or without adequate planning, cost overruns can become a problem. Then the organization has the choice between a loss of face in canceling a program or expending more money than it can afford to keep it afloat. Small nonprofits rarely have the additional funds to experiment with programs, so any departure from the successful business plan must immediately work out well. When the PI is working with a nonprofit, therefore, it is quite important to maintain a firm sense of the current organizational mission and business plan, as this keeps the organization stable. Departures from the mission or business plan should be made by the organization in response to the appropriate development of the organization as well as community needs, not solely in response to a funding opportunity.

Example 1: A freestanding nonprofit graduate school of psychology applies for an NSF grant to deliver STEM education at the BA and MA levels to nontraditional students. On one hand, this graduate professional school already delivers education to nontraditional students and knows this population well. For example, classes are already conducted on evenings and weekends, and most classes already incorporate online aspects of curriculum delivery. On the other hand, this nonprofit school does not have faculty on staff from the "hard" sciences, such as biology or chemistry. They do not have lab space, and they have never delivered an undergraduate curriculum. *Would this new program be a step too far from the business plan of such a school, or is it a natural extension?*

Example 2: A nonprofit organization started out as a civil rights organization for immigrants—essentially a political action agency. Over time as new grant opportunities became available, this organization, led by a very capable and enthusiastic director, applied and won a great deal of funding. Each new program seemed to be more and more distant from the original idea of the organization; however, the programs did deliver needed assistance to the community. Health care was incorporated as well as violence prevention, educational services, and more. There was never any time for formal expansion of the mission or business plan, because the staff is always chasing grant funding. A new opportunity from the Department of Justice has just been released to provide services to former convicts and the program officer has specifically invited the director to apply. *Is this the time to begin a new program that will bring needed financial resources, or should the organization forego this opportunity and take account of its mission?*

WORKING WITH YOUR SPONSORED PROJECTS OFFICE

Your local sponsored projects staff will probably have a very good idea of potential funders, because they work with academic grants day in and day out. They may already know the average size of awards your school wins, and they may be able to point you toward funders that your college or university regularly works with. When you go to speak to your sponsored projects staff member, be sure to take the time to ask about these general institutional considerations, as they may help you as you plan. For example, if your school is on specific foundation funding lists or PIs from your school are eligible for Academic Research Enhancement Award (AREA) grants from the NIH, you may greatly benefit from this information.

Sponsored projects may be able to offer you access to various funder databases, and they may offer training in grant searching. Some sponsored projects officers email opportunities tailored to faculty and staff interests as well.

WORKING WITH THE CORPORATE AND FOUNDATION RELATIONS OFFICE

Corporate and foundation relations officers often work in terms of relationships they have already built with specific funders. While she may be able to offer grant search assistance, one of the most useful things a good corporate and foundation relations officer can do is relate your project information to her stock of knowledge about the funders she is currently working with. Speaking directly with a corporate and foundation relations officer is therefore extremely important in order to get a sense of what is available and to give her a sense of what you are doing.

Often corporate and foundation relations officers visit large foundations and meet with program officers to discuss current projects happening around the institution. During this kind of meeting the officer is basically pitching a few ideas to see which ones will interest the program officer or foundation board. This list of pitches will not be very long, and the key for the PI with a service project is to be one of these projects.

If the foundation shows interest in your project, you will still have to write a proposal, and it can still be turned down. The chances of acceptance are obviously better when the proposal stems from such an exclusive situation. Sometimes beginning PIs think that this sort of proposal can be less carefully executed; however, the opposite is often the case. When the proposal stems from a relationship with the funder, corporate and foundation relations officers often want perfection as part of an expression of respect to the foundation. Such submissions often must pass through the president's office or another upper administrator's office, and so your work will be assessed by a completely different set of expectations and standards than is usual for research grants.

THE NUTS & BOLTS

1. Two main considerations of funders are their mission or what they want to accomplish in the world and what types of organizations and activities they will fund, meaning how they want to accomplish that mission.

2. University research grant databases are often directed primarily toward STEM (science, technology, engineering, and mathematics) disciplines and therefore social scientists may have to employ filters strategically to acquire useful results.

3. Find information about a foundation from its website, or in a grant opportunity database.

4. Grants.gov is the clearinghouse for federal opportunities and functions as a submission portal for many agencies.

5. When reading grant opportunities, save time and read the eligibility section first. Look for reasons the funder will not fund you before you start considering the funder's mission.

6. You may refine your project to fit funder goals; however, think carefully before you depart from your organization's mission.

EXERCISES: WORKING TOWARD MASTERY

1. Choose two of the categories below and find two relevant opportunities each that are currently available on Grants.gov (for a total of four). Give the agency, Grants.gov, and agency opportunity numbers, opportunity title, maximum or average budget amount, match requirements, length of narrative, formatting requirements for narrative, and one paragraph on the type of project(s) that concern each opportunity:

   - K–12 education
   - Anthropology
   - Economics
   - Higher education
   - Psychology
   - Qualitative research
   - Quantitative research
   - Sociology

2. Using a foundation grant opportunity database (like the Foundation Directory or Guidestar), conduct a search for your project. List the top five foundation opportunities you find, with the best opportunity first. Provide the following information for each one:

   - Foundation name
   - Address
   - URL
   - President, CEO, or chair of the board
   - Contact person
   - Funding range
   - Deadline
   - Why is this a good opportunity?

5

Project Design

INTRODUCTION

If you are reading this book, you are probably a graduate student or faculty member at a college or university, which means you already write quite a bit. You may not be Shakespeare, but you can string a sentence together—and you probably get annoyed when people leave the article out or do not correct typos. So, like most academics, you can write.

The good news about the writing aspect of grant proposals is that it does not require sparkling prose (although that is always helpful). Successful grant proposals require clear communication. The singular importance of clarity in grant writing cannot be overemphasized. If the reviewers cannot figure out what you are proposing, they are not likely to fund your project.

Clarity is produced on several different levels:

- The project must make sense.
- The sections of the proposal must be organized and interrelated effectively.
- Paragraphs must flow easily from one to another.
- The sentences of a paragraph must be arranged in the correct order and must complement each other.
- Sentences must be direct and understandable.
- Grammar must be correct.
- Words must be used appropriately.
- Spelling must be correct.
- There should be no typos.

Although this list may sound obvious, it is not always easy to pull off. For one thing, the more familiar the text is, the more likely you are to overlook small but important items, like transitions or articles. In many cases, the author is so familiar with the project that she fills in the details unconsciously as she reads. This can result in gaps in the argument or insufficient detail for the reader to grasp the project. Putting together a concise, well-written grant proposal narrative is no mean feat.

This chapter will help you with the first three items. We will discuss conceptualizing your project and making decisions that support your vision, by working on project design, research questions, goals, objectives, and activities. Then, we will put the resulting structure on paper through a **logic model,** which is a table, diagram, or flow chart designed to help break out activities and their interrelationships within a project. In the case study right after this chapter, we will apply a project to a logic model so you will have a practical example to consider.

PROJECT DESIGN

Project design is a multi-dimensional process because any project is made up of several interlocking parts that may appear simple but in reality can be quite complex, as answering these few simple questions will demonstrate.

Who?

Who will work on your project? Are you working alone or do you have collaborators? Will other people need to be hired? What will each person do?

What?

What is the purpose of the project? What will it accomplish? What resources will you need to run the project? How will the world be different as a result of this project?

How?

How will this project accomplish its purpose? What is the work process you will use to accomplish project goals?

Where?

Where will your project take place? Do you need space on campus? Do you need a specific space in a specific building, or do you need to acquire space off campus? Whose approval will you need to use the space?

When?

What is your proposed start date? Did you choose that start date in consideration of the academic cycle? Do you need some ramp-up time? Have you considered the likely award date? How much time do you need to accomplish each part of the project?

These questions lead you into project design. As you answer them, consider the things that are required to happen as part of the project versus the things that can change or are negotiable. Try to notice which items affect other items. For example, *where* is always an important question and has ramifications for the rest of the project. Having access to a fully outfitted lab creates one type of condition for the grant, and having to furnish a lab creates another.

After you have answered these questions, you must find a way to convert the project design into a proposal. A logic model (which we will discuss later in the chapter) will help you put your design in order and convert it to a budget and into text.

RESEARCH QUESTIONS

For a research grant, the **research questions** define the project design, of course, because the point of the project is to answer these questions. For this reason, it behooves the PI to create thoughtful, specific, data-driven questions. Good research questions are not written on the fly; they benefit from thoughtful consideration and discussion with colleagues. Take your time and make these questions shine.

The purpose of a research question is to carefully define the study by combining the topic and methodology into a question structure that will be answered effectively by the data. Research questions should be responsive to the literature of the discipline(s) involved. As mentioned in Chapter 1, the best research study is often the next logical step in a particular line of inquiry. The ideal research questions refer to areas that have not been explored, have been incompletely studied, or have a demographic or environmental context that has not been examined. Funded projects do not simply fill gaps in the literature; and yet they are not too far beyond where other scholars are working. Funded projects pose meaningful questions that will drive knowledge forward in ways that many people value.

Of course, there are entire books written on the development of proper research questions (see Box 5.3); however, there are four basic problems that are very common to research questions in grant submissions:

1. Open-ended questions

2. Data mismatches

3. Too many questions

4. Incomplete expression

Open-Ended Questions

Open-ended questions can be problematic in a grant proposal because most funders want to know specifics about the investigation in advance. The question should define the form of the answer; the question should inform the reader about what the answer will be. In fact, the question should provide information about what data will answer it properly. For example, you can ask the following open-ended question:

1. Why aren't students interested in pursuing STEM majors?

Or you can ask the question more specifically:

2. Is there a specific age when student interest in STEM subjects drops off? If so, what is the age?

There are many problems with Question 1. For example, how would one know when an answer had been found? It is so open-ended that you could pursue many different approaches to answering it. On the other hand, Question 2 provides a partial answer to Question 1: It asks whether students are interested at younger ages and at what point their interest drops off. The data to be pursued is suggested in the question. You could also ask this question:

3. What factors do non-STEM major students cite when asked why they do not study a STEM subject?

Question 3 provides a sense of how the question will be answered.

Because closed-ended questions most often lead to measurable research outcomes, external funders have a reputation for preferring quantitative studies. Of course, qualitative research can be just as empirical as quantitative work. Whether your research is quantitative or qualitative, the key to obtaining funding is to ask a question that can be answered with data—whether that consists of the demographics of Spanish-speaking immigrants, assessing networks of dental hygienists, or coding classroom dialog between math teachers and their students.

Box 5.1 True Story

As a research administrator, I have seen numerous situations where investing time and effort at the front end of grant development would have saved time, effort, and stress during the submission process. Without careful planning, a team can overlook extremely important aspects of the project, resulting in major budget reformulations and inconvenient rewrites at the last minute. For example, there was a Department of Education proposal where the PIs forgot to factor in pay for teacher-participants' afterschool effort. We discovered this three days before submission.

Thirty teachers would be working an extra 80 hours each per year, and their pay averaged about $38 per hour: $38 × 80 hours × 30 teachers = $91,200 per year.

Of course when working with salary, fringe benefits are also required, and this added about $29,700 for a total of $121,296 to the budget over the maximum request—so cuts had to be made to other lines of the project.

The process of cutting more than $100,000 from the budget caused important revisions to the project plan—the PIs simply could not afford to do some of the things they had originally planned to do. As a result of these cuts, the narrative had to be rewritten to reflect the changed project. Of course, three days from submission, one should be submitting the proposal. Any rewrites at this point should be last-minute sculpting of the text to make it shine rather than a complete revision.

If we had employed better planning and even a logic model at the front end, this crisis could have been averted.

Data Mismatches

Trying to answer a question with data can reveal when a research question is not worded well. For example, if I ask the following question, I may run into some problems figuring out what data to use to answer it:

Do graduate students find grant writing class boring?

How does one define "boring"? *Merriam Webster* says that it is "the state of being weary and restless through lack of interest." How does one quantify this definition? How can weariness or restlessness be measured? Perhaps I could do the following:

- Observe students during class and record how often they engage in off-task behaviors during a lecture
- Code the interactions between students and teachers to track for students' expressed lack of interest
- Have a research assistant sit in the back of the classroom and count the number of laptops displaying screens unrelated to the class topic
- Create a survey that measures students' opinions on their engagement with the grant writing curriculum

Choosing a data-gathering method allows us to specify the question and perhaps conceptualize it differently.

- Do students express lack of engagement behaviorally in grant writing class?
- How do students think about their engagement with the grant writing curriculum?

Box 5.2   Good Advice

If you only remember one thing from this book, remember to always, always follow directions!

Too Many Questions

It is very common to find a plethora of questions in the proposals of new PIs. They may ask as many as five or six different research questions—perhaps because they want to get a lot done with the grant money, or perhaps because they do not know which question will work best and they want to be sure to produce significant results. The problem with too many questions can be either (a) they are repetitive and should be collapsed efficiently into one question, or (b) they represent several different projects and therefore should be proposed separately.

The research question should represent the main thrust of the research, but it does not have to reflect every single nuance: That is what the proposal is for. It often happens that during the process of a research study, interesting information not directly related to the research question is produced. This may be reflected in the proposal rather than the research questions, or it may not be discussed at all.

For example, below is a list of research questions to revise:[1]

- Does the use of acupuncture help speed recovery for drug addicts?
- Do regular acupuncture treatments help addicts resist relapse?
- Do recovering drug addicts from underserved populations report benefits from weekly acupuncture treatment?
- Does daily yoga practice provide psychological benefits for drug addicts in the initial recovery period?
- Does daily yoga practice provide benefits to drug addicts in residential recovery facilities?
- Does daily yoga practice shorten the recovery period?

How many projects can you find in these questions?
I find at least two different projects:

1. Acupuncture to treat recovering drug addicts

    - Does the use of acupuncture help drug addicts speed recovery?
    - Do regular acupuncture treatments help addicts resist relapse?
    - Do recovering drug addicts from underserved populations report benefits from weekly acupuncture treatment?

2. Yoga to treat recovering drug addicts

    - Does daily yoga practice provide psychological benefits for drug addicts in the initial recovery period?
    - Does daily yoga practice provide benefits to drug addicts in residential recovery facilities?
    - Does daily yoga practice shorten the recovery period?

If we read the questions carefully, there are really three different projects in each category. In this case one could opt for multiple projects rather than trying to fit so much work into one project. To answer one really good question is a worthy goal for any proposal.

---

[1] I have left these research questions a little lean to make them easy to compare. Every one of them would require further development to actually function as a research question.

Box 5.3   Resources on Research Questions

This book covers research questions only in a very general way and only from the perspective of grant writing. Readers who desire more assistance in developing effective research questions might look to the following resources or ask an advisor.

Carey, S. S. (2011). *A beginner's guide to scientific method*. Boston: Wadsworth.

Creswell, John W. (2014). *Research design: Qualitative, quantitative, and mixed methods approaches*. Thousand Oaks, CA: Sage.

Frankfort-Nachmias, C., & Nachmias, D. (2007). *Research methods in the social sciences study guide*. New York: Worth Publishers.

Neuman, W. L. (2004). *Basics of social research: Qualitative and quantitative approaches*. Boston: Pearson Education.

Remler, D. K., & Van Ryzin, G. (2001). *Research methods in practice*. Thousand Oaks, CA: Sage.

Salkind, N. J. (2012). *100 questions (and answers) about research methods*. Thousand Oaks, CA: Sage.

Turabian, K. L. (2007). *A manual for writers of research papers, theses, and dissertations: Chicago style for students and researchers* (7th ed.). Chicago: University of Chicago Press.

Incomplete Expression

Another issue for many research questions is that of incomplete expression, meaning that the question does not include all of the relevant facts. Consider the following examples:

Does university faculty intervention assist teachers in providing accurate science instruction to students?

This question sounds academic, but what does it mean? For example, what intervention is being studied? Which faculty will be involved?

Does university science faculty ~~intervention~~ modeling assist teachers in providing accurate science instruction to students?

Then the questions become, what teachers, what students?

Does university science faculty modeling for <u>elementary school</u> teachers assist teachers in providing accurate science instruction to <u>their</u> students?

Then the question emerges, what does accurate science instruction mean? How would this be measured? One way might be to record teacher lectures and analyze them in terms of science content. A less expensive method would be to look at pre- and posttesting of students. Because the measurement of data needs to shape the research question, this would be included.

Does university science faculty modeling for elementary school teachers assist teachers <u>in supporting enhanced academic performance by their students as measured by pre- and posttesting</u>?

GOALS, OBJECTIVES, ACTIVITIES

Some federal funders (like the U.S. Department of Education) will require project **goals** or overarching, long-term, hoped-for accomplishments in addition to (or rather than) research questions. These goals need to be very carefully defined and related to **objectives** (the organizational structures that accomplish the goals) and **activities** (tasks that are carried out to accomplish the objectives). Each activity is related to an objective, which is related to a goal. Defining these is a good practice, because it helps the PI to consider the entirety of the project effort during the planning stage. In fact, defining goals, objectives, and activities is the basis for the logic model introduced a little later in this chapter.

Goals

Creating goals can be a little tricky, because the definition of goals and objectives are often confused by both funders and PIs alike. *Merriam Webster* defines *goal* as the "end towards which effort is directed," synonymous with *aim*. So the goal is the long-term result of the project—which, with research, is generally the testing of a hypothesis. For a service project, a goal is often a benefit projected to result from the intervention. It might be to send more underserved high school students to college, to increase reading scores for K–6 students, or to lessen alcohol consumption on campus. Notice these are measurable goals: The number of high school students who go to college can be counted; students' reading scores can be determined; and likewise, the number of DUIs, disorderly conduct situations, or students seeking counseling can be counted. Like research questions linked to the resulting data, measurable goals are preferred because they can be quantified.

Often the goals are created to define project success. For example, how would success be measured for a program designed to help first-generation college students excel at the university? If success for first-generation college students is defined as retention to a program or to the university, then the goals will involve retention and be stated something like this: "As a result of this project, participating first-generation college students will be more likely than nonparticipants to finish their degrees within six years," or even, "First-generation participants will be 50 percent more likely than nonparticipants to enroll in university classes the semester following the intervention." On the other hand, success for first-generation college students may be defined as integration to the university community as reflected by involvement in school activities. Such a goal might read something like this: "First-generation student participants will be more likely than nonparticipants to join university activities and clubs during their first year at the university."

Box 5.4 The Nuts & Bolts: Using Funder Language

It is important to keep in mind that different funders may require different terms to describe goal-creating activities; or they may define terms differently. For example, "goals" and "objectives" may appear interchangeable in an RFP. One funder might require the term "goal"; another funder might use a totally different term, like "aim."

Be alert for the type of terminology the funder uses. Make sure you understand it and use it appropriately—meaning, in the way the funder uses it.

Objectives and Activities

Objectives are the organizational structures that make up the project, which are themselves composed of activities. These are all created to accomplish the goals. For example, if I was proposing a project to increase retention of first-generation college students, I might set a goal to increase their academic success by improving their pass rate. One way to accomplish this might be to provide tutoring services. That would be an objective or a real-world solution to help achieve the goal. Then, in order to accomplish this objective, I could define the activities necessary to create the tutoring services. The process could be thought of as diagrammed in Figure 5.1. Each goal can have multiple objectives, and each objective can have multiple activities. Conversely, every activity must fit into at least one objective, and every objective must fit into at least one goal.

Activities require resources and make up the budget. When relating activities to the budget, ask these kinds of questions:

- How many tutors will we hire?
- How much will we pay them?
- How many hours will they work each week?
- Can work-study funds be used to help defray this cost?

Is this a kind of logic model? Yes, absolutely.

Figure 5.1   Enhancing Academic Success

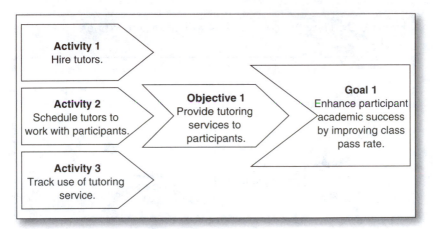

Each activity builds the objective, and the objective builds the goal.

LOGIC MODELS

One of the best tools for relating project structure to a grant proposal is the logic model, which is a kind of schematic or diagram of the project. Creating a logic model is an efficient way to conceptualize the project as well as all the resources that will be required for successful completion, from start to finish.

One strength of the logic model is its clear application to the budget. During logic model development, the resources required to run the project can be analyzed and listed out. This list, of course, will transfer directly to the budget for itemization and costing. By figuring out all the necessary resources during the development of the logic model, you ensure that all budget lines are related to project objectives and goals and, therefore, that all project objectives and goals will be sufficiently funded for implementation.

Analyzing the budget and project process through a logic model will assist in the creation of the proposal narrative in two ways:

1. The entire project description will be worked out without the demands of narrative creation, allowing the PI to consider how the project will work best in a straightforward way.

2. Working out the kinks of the project before the narrative process begins is more likely to prevent painful and unnecessary rewrites (and budget revisions) toward submission time.

Figure 5.2   How the Logic Model Relates to the Proposal

Project Idea

Narrative

Logic Model

Resources
(needed and
in hand)

Budget

Narrative and budget are based
on the logic model and reflect
each other directly.

The logic model brings order to ideas and resources, helping to create a better project.

The logic model, rather than the narrative, becomes the central organizing document of the submission.

Many people design the project as they write it, making the narrative the organizing document in grant writing, yet this is not efficient for several reasons:

- It is difficult to glance at a narrative and quickly see its elements, making the project more difficult to reorganize.
- If the project organization is worked out through the narrative this means that the organizing information is buried in the text, and therefore challenging to find and update.
- When the project is organized through the narrative, it is difficult to be sure that all project components are accounted for in the budget.

On the other hand, when items are listed out in a table or graphically arranged, it is much easier to conceptualize the relationship of ideas and to create alternative logical arrangements of them.

Theoretically, a logic model can include whatever categories you need to clarify your thinking about your project. When you are trying to design a project, especially for a university grant, you are using the logic model to apply your thinking to project creation in an institutional context. In that case, I recommend that your model include research questions/goals, interventions/objectives, activities, and resources.

USING A LOGIC MODEL

Perhaps a van is needed to conduct a project. If the project is being designed by writing the narrative, the PI might end up with a sentence like this:

> Participants will be taken to the afterschool program in a van so that they can begin training as environmental science interns. The onsite internship program will consist of four different labs located in the main school building.

The writer mentions the van in passing and moves on to the afterschool program, the focus of the project. The problem is that if the van is only mentioned in this one sentence, buried on Page 7 of a 15-page narrative, it may be overlooked and never find its way into the budget. That would be an important omission.

If, instead, the PI was working with a logic model, she could write the following:

Research Question	Intervention/ Objectives	Activities	Resources
		Transport students to afterschool program.	

Having a column to the right for resources is pretty handy, because it prompts the writer to think, what do I need to transport the participants? The answer to that question is what goes in the resources field. In this case, what is needed is a van. Then, because this is planning, the PI might think, what other resources do I need to have a van for the project? Do I need a driver, insurance, or a garage? Should I ask for sales tax in addition to the van price? The table allows the PI to think about the van in some important detail.

Research Question	Intervention/ Objectives	Activities	Resources
		Transport students to afterschool program.	Purchase a van (grant) Check on • Driver (add a grant-funded employee?) • Insurance • Parking spot • Sales tax

For those who would like to include a more complex and theoretical logic model in the narrative, there are many interesting books available to consider; however, for simple project planning I recommend the (free) logic model system produced by the W. K. Kellogg Foundation. It is available on their website (www .wkkf.org); search using the key words "logic model."

For more information on how to create and use a logic model, see Case Study 1: Application of a Logic Model.

WORKING WITH YOUR SPONSORED PROJECTS OFFICE

Your sponsored projects personnel will probably appreciate efforts to use a logic model to design your project. They regularly see projects submitted that are not well thought out and, therefore, do not get funded.

The average sponsored projects officer knows a great deal about how his institution works and may also know something about project planning. If the office is designed to provide project assistance, take advantage of the knowledge the staff may offer. Among other things, your sponsored projects staff may be able to discuss the following:

- Projects that have been successfully funded from your institution. What has worked for other PIs may also work for you.
- Problems that other PIs at your institution have faced and how you might design your project to deal with or avoid these.
- What sorts of specific complications may be caused by your project plan, and how to work these out effectively.

Your sponsored projects officer may be able to recommend people in various departments to contact if you need to enlist their help for your project.

THE NUTS & BOLTS

1. Good project design requires robust research questions or goals, and it is helped along by the application of a logic model.

2. Robust research questions can be answered with data, are created in consideration of the literature, are focused, and are few in number.

3. Project goals are overarching, measurable statements of the long-term aims of the project; objectives are administrative structures, made up of activities that drive the goals forward.

4. Use a logic model to help design and organize the project so that the budget and narrative reflect each other.

EXERCISES: WORKING TOWARD MASTERY

1. Create a research question or hypothesis for your project. Follow your disciplinary guidelines, and be sure that the question is clear and complete, based on the literature, measurable, and potentially of interest to a funder.

2. Create a logic model for a project based on this question. Follow the guidance provided in this chapter, as well as Case Study 1: Application of a Logic Model. Be sure to include goals, objectives, activities, and resources in a simple format, such as the following example:

Goals	Objectives	Activities	Resources

CHAPTER TERMS

Activities: Tasks that make up the objectives. Each activity is related to an objective, which is related to a goal. Ideally, each activity is represented on the budget, either as part of the request or as match.

Goals: The abstract, long-term, hoped-for accomplishments of the project, also called *aims*.

Logic model: A table, diagram, or flow chart designed to help break out activities and their interrelationships within a project. Logic models come in many varieties and can be used for many purposes.

Objectives: The organizational structures that push goals forward. Objectives are composed of activities.

Research question: A carefully defined question that combines the topic and methodology in a question structure that will be answered effectively by data.

CASE STUDY 1

Application of a Simple Logic Model

It is all very well to talk about logic models and how wonderful they are, but what does that really mean? What does it look like to design a project using a logic model, and how would you convert the result into a narrative and a budget?

This case study will start with the development of one research question for a community service project and the application of the research question to a simple logic model. It will then adapt the logic model to the project using the goal/objective/activity style of working as an example of using the logic model for a service project. Then we will develop a narrative outline and part of a budget using the result.

The example project is designed to assist under-resourced families deal with credit and finance issues more effectively. Perhaps based on the literature and observation we hypothesize that credit counseling would help these families manage their financial situations better. We decide to test this by providing services and measuring the results in terms of effects on the families.

LOGIC MODEL USING A RESEARCH QUESTION

Research Question

Of course, we start with the research question. Here is what we have so far. Read it and think about what you might do to improve it.

Does credit counseling help under-resourced families manage their finances more effectively?

This is not very well defined in this question, is it? What does "manage their finances more effectively" mean? Does it mean avoiding foreclosure, saving money, or avoiding bankruptcy? Perhaps it means all of these things. Getting data on a savings account will probably be difficult; however, data on the presence of catastrophic financial situations may be less personal for participants to report.[1]

Does credit counseling help under-resourced families ~~manage their finances more effectively~~ avoid major financial disruptions?

This data will be probably be easier to manage and measure: Participants will simply be asked whether they have undergone major financial disruptions at follow-up. We must be sure to define "major financial disruptions" in the methodology section.

Now the question is, should we just be looking at under-resourced families? Perhaps there are many under-resourced families that are at risk for financial disruption based on their low socioeconomic status (SES) rather than lack of information. Credit counseling probably will not help much with this. Perhaps the project should seek at-risk families, those who are behind in their mortgages, credit card payments, or considering bankruptcy at whatever income level is presented.

Does credit counseling help ~~under-resourced~~ at-risk families avoid major financial disruptions?

Naturally there are many ways to change this research question to make it ready to pull the weight of a project. Some people prefer more detail, others less; however, we will proceed with this version of the research question for this case study.

Does credit counseling help at-risk families avoid major financial disruptions?

In working with a research question, I would adapt the first column of the logic model to read "Research Question" but leave the other columns intact.

Research Question	Objectives	Activities	Resources
1. **Does credit counseling help at-risk families avoid major financial disruptions?**			

---

[2]Of course, if I was actually carrying out this study, I would go to the literature and find out how others had measured improvement of the family financial situation.

Objectives

Objectives are still the structural organization of activities that are actually performed, and in this case they drive the performance of the investigation of the research question. What objectives do we need to accomplish to answer this question with data? The first thing would be to provide credit counseling to families. But which families? Where do we find them? We need a recruitment plan, so I will add that to my logic model.

Next we consider providing credit counseling, the central objective of the project, and then consider how to build data-gathering processes into the proposal.

Research Question	Interventions/ Objectives	Activities	Resources
1. Does credit counseling help at-risk families avoid major financial disruptions?	A. Recruit at-risk families.		
	B. Provide credit counseling to participant families.		
	C. Gather data on project efficacy.		

Activities

What activities will we do to accomplish the objectives and therefore accomplish the goal?

For Item 1A, the question is, how do we recruit at-risk families? Have we even defined *at-risk* yet? That might tell us a lot about where we would conduct outreach. For now, let's agree that we will need to perform some basic recruitment tasks:

- Define what we mean by *at-risk* and create minimum levels of risk to receive services.
- Publicize study services in appropriate magazines, online, and with organizations serving at-risk families.
- Create a greeting process where participants will be welcomed and oriented to the study.

Item 1B, considering the issue of the credit counseling services, brings up entirely new questions. Who will provide the services? Where will they provide them? What is the study plan in terms of how many hours of assistance participating families receive? These questions form the basis of the intervention, and perhaps we have not yet worked the details out. In this case, we can include some notes and build on the project as we figure it out:

- Decide who the credit counselors will be.
- Acquire office space at a downtown university campus to provide services.
- Determine how many hours of assistance participants will receive.

Finally, we must think about data gathering for the project. Again, at this early stage we may not have things worked out; however, we know generally what must be done:

- Seek an external evaluator.
- Create a data-gathering plan.
- Among project staff, decide who will be responsible for data gathering and input.

Here is how the model might look so far.

Research Question	Intervention/ Objectives	Activities	Resources
1. Does credit counseling help at-risk families avoid major financial disruptions?	A. Recruit at-risk families.	i. **Define what we mean by** *at-risk* **and create minimum levels of risk to receive services.** ii. **Publicize study services in appropriate magazines, online, and with organizations serving at-risk families.** iii. **Create a greeting process where participants will be welcomed and oriented to the study.**	

Research Question	Intervention/ Objectives	Activities	Resources
	B. Provide credit counseling to participant families.	i. Define who the credit counselors will be. ii. Acquire office space at a downtown university campus to provide services. iii. Determine how many hours of assistance participants will receive.	
	C. Gather data on project efficacy and/or evaluation.	i. Seek an external evaluator. ii. Create a data-gathering plan. iii. Determine who will be responsible for data gathering and input.	

Of course, as project planning proceeds, we will use this table to record additional detail. For example, once we figure out who will be doing the data gathering and input, we will record the position for Item 1Ciii.

Resources

Next, resources should be considered. What will we need to accomplish each activity? At this stage, it is best to consider all resources, including those that exist already or that your organization is providing, meaning match. Although you may not even tell the funder your institution will be providing this match or cost share, you, as the PI, should be quite aware of it, because you may need to confirm it with your university or college before you can make it part of your grant.

So, next to each activity category consider the resources that are required to carry out the activity, whether they exist in your organization already, whether you have access to them, and whether you will include them in your request to the funder. In areas where we do not know what the resources will be yet, we can put TBD (to be determined).

Research Question	Intervention/ Objectives	Activities	Resources
1. Does credit counseling help at-risk families avoid major financial disruptions?	A. Recruit at-risk families.	i. Define what we mean by *at-risk* and create minimum levels of risk to receive services.	TBD
		ii. Publicize study services in appropriate magazines, online, and with organizations serving at-risk families.	**How much do ads in magazines and online cost?**
		iii. Create a greeting process where participants will be welcomed and oriented to the study.	TBD
	B. Provide credit counseling to participant families.	i. Define who the credit counselors will be.	**How many will be needed?** **How much will they make per year?**
		ii. Acquire office space at a downtown university campus to provide services.	**Who do we ask about this?**
		iii. Determine how many hours of assistance participants will receive.	TBD
	C. Gather data on project efficacy and/or evaluation.	i. Seek an external evaluator.	**How much will the evaluator charge?**
		ii. Create a data-gathering plan.	TBD
		iii. Determine who will be responsible for data gathering or input.	**Do we have to hire a new person or add this to the grad RA duties?**

LOGIC MODEL USING GOALS

If we are creating a service project and are not interested in pursuing a research question, we simply formulate the research question as a goal. A good goal has a very similar structure to a research question; it should be specific and measurable.

Goal: Provide credit counseling to help at-risk families avoid major financial disruptions.

Then we would make a few changes to the table.

GOAL	Objectives	Activities	Resources
1. **Provide credit counseling to help at-risk families avoid major financial disruptions.**	A. Recruit at-risk families.	i. Define what we mean by *at-risk* and create minimum levels of risk to receive services.	TBD
		ii. Publicize study services in appropriate magazines, online, and with organizations serving at-risk families.	How much do ads in magazines and online cost?
		iii. Create a greeting process where participants will be welcomed and oriented to the study.	TBD
	B. Provide credit counseling to participant families.	i. Who will the credit counselors be?	How many will be needed? How much will they make per year?
		ii. Acquire office space at a downtown university campus to provide services.	Who do we ask about this?
		iii. Determine how many hours of assistance participants will receive.	TBD
	C. Gather data on project efficacy and/or evaluation.	i. Seek an external evaluator.	How much will the evaluator charge?
		ii. Create a data-gathering plan.	TBD
		iii. Determine who will be responsible for data gathering and input.	Do we have to hire a new person or add this to the grad RA duties?

USING THE LOGIC MODEL TO CREATE A NARRATIVE

Once fully filled out, the logic model can be used to create different sections of the narrative, especially the project description. Logic models are enormously helpful here because it is easy for the writer to elide important details when he is working from memory. One can forget the specifics, and one can also feel that they are so obvious that they do not need to be mentioned. Unfortunately, what is obvious to the PI may not be obvious to others, particularly not to the reviewers who only have the benefit of the proposal to inform them about the project. The logic model brings all the details to the view of the writer, allowing him to pick and choose which ones to include, exclude, and highlight.

The wonderful thing about this particular logic model is that it provides the outline structure automatically, especially if you remember to letter and number each entry.

1. Provide credit counseling to help at-risk families avoid major financial disruptions.

    A. Recruit at-risk families.

        i. Define what we mean by *at-risk* and create minimum levels of risk to receive services.

        ii. Publicize study services in appropriate magazines, online, and with organizations serving at-risk families.

        iii. Create a greeting process where participants will be welcomed and oriented to the study.

    B. Provide credit counseling to participant families.

        i. Define who credit counselors will be.

        i. Acquire office space at a downtown university campus to provide services.

        ii. Define how many hours of assistance participants will receive.

    C. Gather data on project efficacy and/or evaluation.

        i. Seek an external evaluator.

        ii. Create a data-gathering plan.

        iii. Determine who will be responsible for data gathering and input.

Now I can begin writing a project description based on this structure.

To accomplish the project goal of [1][2] providing credit counseling to help at-risk families avoid major financial disruptions, project personnel will engage in three main program areas: [1A] recruitment, [1B] credit counseling, and [1C] program data collection.

The project defines [1Ai] at-risk families according to the following indicators, as defined by Ralph Smith in his 2012 study [indicate risk factors]. As such, families with the following risk factors will be recruited to the project and provided services:

- Job loss of an adult
- Chronic illness or death of job-holding adult
- Recent divorce
- Unmarried parent

[1Aii] Participants will be recruited through advertising as well as through contacts with social service agencies. . . .

We can write through this entire outline and create a clear, structured project description that will convey to the reviewers exactly what the project will entail. Then we can use the resources column to organize the budget.

USING THE LOGIC MODEL TO CREATE A BUDGET

Similarly, the logic model can be used to create a list of expenses or a budget for the project. Just copy and paste the Activities and Resources columns into a spreadsheet where they begin the budget. Add a Budget Lines column, and you will have begun the two tasks that most often seem insurmountable to the new PI: writing your narrative and creating your budget. We will dedicate two chapters each to budget and narrative development over the next four chapters.

---

[2]All information in brackets is included to assist understanding of the reader and would not be included in an actual proposal.

Activities	Resources	Budget Lines
i. Define what we mean by at-*risk* and create minimum levels of risk to receive services.	TBD	TBD
ii. Publicize study services in appropriate magazines, online, and with organizations serving at-risk families.	How much do ads in magazines and online cost?	Ad on Craig's List = ? Ad in local newspaper = ? Google ad = ?
iii. Create a greeting process where participants will be welcomed and oriented to the study.	TBD	TBD
i. Define who the credit counselors will be.	How many will be needed? How much will they make per year?	2 credit counselors × $45,000 × 2 years Add fringe benefits.
ii. Acquire office space at a downtown university campus to provide services.	Who do we ask about this?	Will this be free, or will the project need to pay rent, electricity, water, parking?
iii. Define how many hours of assistance participants will receive.	TBD	TBD
i. Seek an external evaluator.	How much will the evaluator charge?	$5,000 × 2 years
ii. Create a data-gathering plan.	TBD	TBD
iii. Who will be responsible for data gathering and input?	Do we have to hire a new person or add this to the grad RA duties?	Extra RA at $12,550 + tuition × 2 years

6

Budgeting 101

What do you think about when someone says "grant writing?" If you are like most people, you think about writing a narrative, pounding out paragraphs of text, and wordsmithing. Few people associate grant writing with budgets, even though budgeting is an intrinsic part of the process. In fact, many PIs avoid budgeting their projects until the last minute.

Of course, there are perfectly good reasons to avoid budgeting:

- People may not know where to get the estimates to properly cost out the items they will need for the project.
- Some people may not be very comfortable with math.
- Other people may have been told that budgeting should come after the narrative.

It is far better to get the budget done early.

It is easier to revise the budget in a spreadsheet format, when there is little or no narrative to adjust, than to wait until the narrative is in its final stages. Picking through a developed narrative to figure out what needs to change with the revised budget can be difficult. If any points are missed, then the narrative will not reflect the budget, which will pose problems.

University grants tend to require multiple approvals before submission. The primary (but not sole) document involved in the approvals will be the budget.

Having the budget done early and making sure that it is properly aligned with early drafts of the narrative will allow the approval process to proceed on schedule and help minimize last-minute scrambles to submit.

The costing process may involve some research. For example, how are course remissions priced? Under what conditions can an administrative assistant be hired? Who purchases the desk and computer setup for new hires? What are indirect costs and how should they be applied? Getting the answers to these questions may take longer than the beginning PI will imagine. Starting early can help.

GENERAL BUDGET CONSIDERATIONS

Whatever type of budget you are working on and whatever sort of funder it will be submitted to, the same general guidance for budget preparation operates. Read the RFP or guidelines thoroughly. Follow directions. Present as much information as you can as clearly as possible. Here are a few other important thoughts to consider:

- **Your institution is liable for the grant award.** That means that any problem with the budget could mean your employer will be forced to make an unplanned expenditure—for example, unbudgeted shipping costs, unforeseen match, or even a returned award. This sort of financial risk is the reason why your sponsored projects office may be very strict about proposal budgets.
- **Every budget should be costed out thoroughly for every submission.** Costing out each budget carefully will ensure that your project is funded at the appropriate level and will prevent the risk of unplanned expenditures. Further, a thoughtful budget demonstrates that the PI is organized, a good planner, and has a grasp on the reality of implementation.
- **A budget should only include expenses that are necessary for the project proposed.** This means that while budgeting for Project A one cannot include costs for (unrelated) Project B—even though Project B may have its own gaps and challenges, it might be very worthwhile or it may involve substantially the same team. Likewise, a budget cannot include lines to pay for unrelated institution expenses, even when these expenses are real and dire. For example, you cannot funnel grant funds into the department to replace an old copier or to buy yourself a laptop just because the institution has not done so.

Box 6.1　Federal Budgeting

Because all federal agencies use similar budgeting standards, this book will most often follow general federal guidelines in discussion of budgets. Instances where foundation and federal budgets may differ will be highlighted and discussed along the way. A budget for a foundation that follows federal guidelines may be considered a little more detailed than necessary; however following federal guidelines is an assurance to foundations that your institution follows a higher form of accountability than most foundations are in a position to enforce.

Costing Items Out

Each budget line must be properly **costed out.** This means that each item should be described in some detail, including the per unit expense, the number of units, tax, shipping, installation, and so forth. Funders may ask for a **budget narrative** or **justification**, which is a document that details how the cost was arrived at and its importance to the project (see Case Study 3 on creating a budget narrative). This kind of detail is normal for federal submissions, and even when a foundation does not request it, the staff is generally happy to see well-thought-out, detailed budget lines.

Match or Cost Sharing

There are times when the college or university chooses to contribute its own resources toward a grant project. When this is planned and occurs at the budgeting stage, it is called **cost sharing** or **match**. When funders require a match from the institution in order to compete for the award, this is called *involuntary cost sharing*.

Some colleges and universities have ample matching funds available, and others may resist putting cost share up for various reasons. At many institutions, a match is only provided if the proposal is built around a very good idea that lines up with current thinking about the direction of the institutional mission. Acquiring cost share for a specific project may be a balancing act between finding the appropriate resources available, making the project relevant to those who have control over the resources, and determining what is next in the organization's development.

Match can be a delicate negotiation for the PI, so here are a few ideas to consider when dealing with match requirements:

Grapple with the requirement until you really understand what it means for your project and your situation, even if you must call the funder for more information. For example, is it a one-to-one (1:1) or a one-to-two (1:2) match? Does the match include indirect costs at the institutional rate? Is the match limited to the college or university or can it be contributed by partner institutions as well?

Ask your institution for what is needed and keep asking until you get a definite yes or no. Unclear or incomplete answers may mean that the topic is still under consideration.

Be ready to compromise. This is a negotiation.

Stay on top of how the match affects the project and what it requires of the institution, as these considerations can quickly shift.

Understand that if your institution refuses a required match, you cannot submit the proposal. As frustrating as this may be, try to treat it as a learning experience and move on to the next opportunity. Sometimes failed negotiations can create awareness of the need for matching resources and result in better outcomes with later proposals.

Box 6.2 The Nuts & Bolts:
Why Funders Require Match or Cost Share

Many funders require matching funds from the institution, and they have a range of purposes for doing this. Some feel that institutional match demonstrates commitment to the project and elicits better stewardship. Others are attempting to make their awards go farther or award to a larger number of projects.

Match has a tendency to modulate the tendency toward bloated requests. This is particularly true of certain potentially large grants that require match in the language of one-to-one or two-to-one. For a one-to-one match the institution would have to put in one dollar for every dollar the funder awards. With a two-to-one match, the college or university would pledge two dollars for every dollar the funder contributes. These sorts of ratios effectively prevent small organizations from requesting overly large awards since a $1 million award with one-to-one match would require the institution to come up with $1 million toward the project as well. The project's true total budget in this case will be $2 million.

The Budget Maximum

The **request** is the total amount of money you will ask for in the proposal. The request is very often governed by what the funder has indicated is appropriate, and this should be carefully kept in mind during grant planning. In other words, if the award has a cap, this will limit what you can put into your budget, and therefore it will probably limit your plans. A $10,000 project is not the same as a $100,000 project, after all.

Sometimes figuring out how much to request is not easy because an exact dollar amount is not given in the guidelines.

When There Is an Award Maximum

Obviously, when the funder is very specific, stating in the award section of an RFP that, for example, 10 awards of a total of $250,000 will be offered, the PI should limit the budget to $250,000. In this case you could ask for $249,999, not $250,001.

When There Is an Award Range

An RFP may offer a range—for example, from $50,000 to $250,000. In this case you might choose to make a request somewhere in the middle of that range, although you could certainly ask for an amount up to the maximum.

When the Total Dollar Amount and the Number of Awards Are Given

A funder may state, for example, that 10 grants for a total of $2.5 million will be awarded. The total amount will divide such that the awards will average around $250,000 each. In this case, it probably will not make much difference if the request is $245,765 or $258,928. A budget of $50,000 as well as a budget of $2 million can be submitted; however, these totals reflect widely divergent project capacity. In this case it is especially necessary to check the size of previous awards. If a look at the last three years of funding reveals that awards generally ranged from $25,000 to $75,000, a strategic PI will keep the request generally within these bounds.

As in all grant writing matters, the budget is often a question of context and balance.

Box 6.3 The Nuts & Bolts: Foundation Requests

When looking at a foundation's past grants, you may see many small awards of from $5,000 to $50,000, with a few larger awards of $100,000 or $200,000 peppered throughout the list. If you research the funder's history, you will probably learn that

(Continued)

(Continued)

the large awards are given to organizations in developed relationships with that foundation, while the small awards are reserved for new, less-familiar organizations. Unless indicated otherwise by a program officer, it would be best to keep your first request to such a foundation in line with the more typical, lower awards.

Underfunded Budgets

There are PIs who believe that lower requests are desirable. In effect, they are hoping to beat the competition by providing similar services at a lower cost. Some funders will decline a project if the budget does not seem to be effectively costed out. Other funders will agree that they are getting a "good deal" and may fund in spite of an underfunded budget. Therefore, the underfunding strategy or making the lowest request possible can lead to one of two undesirable outcomes for the PI:

1. Loss of award because the budget is not appropriately costed out

2. Having to administer an underfunded project

Underfunded projects are a problem for the PI because although he may have received an award, he has now promised to administer a project whether or not there is enough money to get the work done. Perhaps the project really needed 200 hours of data input assistance or an administrative coordinator even though the PI did not budget these lines. Who will fill these gaps? The PI is ultimately responsible for making sure the work is accomplished, so he is generally the one who must find a way to fill the gaps.

More than one PI has been awarded a project that is ultimately unmanageable because the budget is underfunded. If you ever find yourself in this situation, there are three things that can be done:

1. Go back to the funder and ask for more money.

This works best when the funder helped make the decisions that led to underfunding—for example, requesting a very specific set of tasks and offering an award far too small to get the work done. If you must request a larger award, do this in consultation with your sponsored projects office.

2. Lean on the institution.

This is generally not a welcome move from the point of view of the university, and while some help may be provided for one project, the habitual underfunding of projects will be noticed and can become a problem for the PI. For small institutions, having to provide extra funds to see a project completed can be highly destabilizing.

3. As the PI, contribute more uncompensated time and effort.

Any experienced PI will testify that all grant projects are hard work and add substantially to one's responsibilities. Having to expend even more effort to make up for underfunding is not going to make the work any easier, more efficient, or more enjoyable.

Common sense says to avoid underfunding by creating a budget to fund the work appropriately. Be honest and do not cut corners. If what is needed surpasses the award available, restructure the project, seek multiple awards, and/or work with the university to create an adequate match.

Box 6.4 True Story

A colleague worked on a project where shipping costs for a large scientific equipment purchase were not factored into the budget. The equipment cost over $100,000, and so perhaps the PI was not thinking about shipping—it probably seemed like a minor consideration. Minor it was, until the bill of about $3,000 came in and someone had to pay. The department ended up picking up the tab. If you were the chair, how would you feel about this unplanned expenditure?

Getting Started

So how do you actually begin a budget? One way would be to go back to Case Study 1 where we discussed how to create a logic model. Notice the resources category: These are the predicted resource needs the project will have. One could just start at the top of the list and cost each item out as a line in the budget.

Open a spreadsheet program, look at your first item, and follow these steps to cost it out.

What is the cost of one of these items?

For most items you can probably get a good ballpark estimate online. If you are working with a vendor, get a quote in writing. For salary or wages, contact human resources for the monthly, biweekly, or hourly rate. It is a good idea to create a file in the project folder and store PDF copies of all your costing sources as the documentation will come in handy when you create your budget justification or when you are asked about your estimates.

The Nuts and Bolts of Calculus at $110 each.

How many of these items do you need?

Keep in mind that if the item is expendable, like survey instruments or workbooks, you may need to purchase these items at multiple times during the grant period.

200 calculus books, *The Nuts and Bolts of Calculus*, $110 × 200 = $22,000.

Is there sales tax?

If so, find out what it is and add it in; however, be specific about what part of the cost is the item and what part is the sales tax.

200 calculus books, *The Nuts and Bolts of Calculus*
($110 × 200) + ($110 × 200 × 8.25%) = $23,815.

Is there a shipping cost?

Get an estimate for this amount and add it in.

200 calculus books, *The Nuts & Bolts of Calculus*
($110 × 200) + ($110 × 200 × 8.25%) = $23,815. Free shipping.

The result is your total for that line.

Once you have costed out all the lines or while you are working on this process, you can put the lines into order. Often the funder furnishes this order by providing you a template. When this is not the case, the following table illustrates a typical order for budget lines.

Section	Typical Lines
1. Personnel	Salaries and wages, including graduate and undergraduate student pay for both the academic year and the summer.
2. Fringe Benefits	A percentage of salary added on to pay for health coverage, life insurance, and other standard employee benefits as well as FICA, social security, and so on. Sponsored projects will know what the fringe rate is for your institution.

Section	Typical Lines
3. Equipment	Federal definition: Nonconsumable items over $5,000 that will last longer than one year. The definition for foundations tends to be more flexible.
4. Travel & Hospitality	Domestic and international travel, including airfare, accommodations, meals & incidental expenses (M&IE), ground travel, catering, meeting space, etc.
5. Materials & Supplies	Books, instructional supplies (that are not part of indirect costs), small electronic equipment (cameras, recording devices), etc.
6. Subcontracts	The costs associated with collaborators at other institutions.
7. Consultants	The evaluator, statistician, or other role providing well-defined services for the grant.
8. Other	Items that do not fit into the other sections.
9. Subtotal	All direct expenses.
10. Indirect Costs	Indirects as a percentage of the subtotal. This is a negotiated percentage for federal grants. For foundations, there may be no indirects or they may be set by the foundation at 10%, 12%, or 15%.
11. Total Request	Subtotal + indirects.

Box 6.5   Doing Your Own Budget

While many PIs work at universities and colleges where a sponsored projects staff member will create the project budget, PIs at other institutions may not receive this kind of assistance. If you must create your own budget, just remember, as with anything else, creating budgets is a matter of learning the basics and then practicing. The most important skills you will need include the ability to run the spreadsheet program and some very basic algebra. Once you have the mechanics down, budgets are not as difficult as they look.

FOUNDATION BUDGETS

Like most things in the foundation world, foundation budget instructions vary. The instructions may be as simple as one sentence, "Submit a budget," or they may last through several pages of text. Budgeting rules tend to appear in the budget section of online forms, but they may also appear in other areas, like the RFP, general guidelines, or perhaps in a specific budget instruction document. It is therefore very important to read ALL funder materials before you begin preparing a foundation budget.

Very few foundations require more detail than the federal model; most (but not all) have fewer rules, offering the proposer options in terms of forms, fonts, style of write-up, and so forth. Although it may seem easier to prepare a budget for a funder with few expressed preferences, this is not necessarily the case, because you may be left wondering how to handle important questions.

Foundation allowable costs may be far more permissive than those of federal funders. Sometimes they will fund events, including fundraising events, food, and lunches, as long as these are proven to support the project objectives. Many foundations appreciate the detail of federal-style costing, so even PIs that work extensively with foundations can benefit from understanding best practices for federal grants.

Box 6.6 The Nuts & Bolts: Foundation Estimates

Federal budget lines are generally given to the cent then rounded up to the dollar, often automatically in the spreadsheet. A federal line might look like this:

Midday sustenance for 30 participants: $19.50 \times 30 = \$585$

In contrast, foundations may prefer rounded numbers, so this entry on a foundation budget may appear as the following:

Lunch for 30 participants: $600

It is still important to arrive at the total by finding out how much the lunch will really cost, then rounding up. You would not want to get caught underfunded in this (or any other) line! For this reason, it can be wise to have an internal budget with the exact costs, and to prepare the foundation request using rounded lines on the basis of internal budget.

CITY, COUNTY, AND STATE BUDGETS

There are 50 states, and so there are, conceivably, a minimum of 50 different budget submission styles for state grants. There are far more than 50 government budgeting styles, however, because each state has a number of counties and cities and each of these can create specific budget requirements. This reality makes it difficult to write at length on submission styles for city, county, and state grant programs: There are simply too many local programs across the United States to provide comprehensive information within this book.

Here are some general tips for submitting to city, county, and state competitions:

- **If you learn the lessons of federal submissions, you should be well prepared** to submit to state and local government entities. Of course, if you follow the first rule, "Follow directions," you should be prepared for any competition.
- **Do not assume that state and local submissions will work just like federal submissions**, even when the funding ultimately comes from a federal agency (i.e., a block grant). Every locality has its own context, tradition, and concerns that can manifest in various submission policies.
- **Local authorities may expect a great deal more documentation** in terms of budget lines and implementation than the federal government does. Be prepared to submit more proof of expenses and more forms.
- **State, county, and city competitions are not always or not completely computerized,** so a paper submission may be involved. If you will be submitting 15 copies of a 200-page proposal, plan early for the kind of office supplies that will be needed for a tidy submission: three-ring binders, labels, tab dividers, and perhaps a new banker's box for delivering the binders.
- **Local grant authorities may be more accessible to you.** You may have more opportunities to ask questions, get tips for submissions, and build relationships with the staff of local agencies. Your local government staffers may relate to your concerns in a more proximal way than federal officers do.

FEDERAL BUDGETS

As noted previously, one of the distinguishing features of federal grants is that the Office of Management and Budget (OMB) makes rules that span the various agencies. This gives federal granting some unifying principles, at least in terms of required documentation and allowable costs. Federal grants do not have the same variety of accounting procedures that local and foundation competitions do, and they are distinguished by some very specific concepts.

Direct and Indirect Costs

Federal budgets are conceptually divided into two sections: direct and indirect costs. The **direct costs** are those that directly fund project activities—for example, books for the participants to use or wages of the tutors who will teach them. Direct costs can be identified, counted, reimbursed, added up in a budget, and requested from the funder.

On the other hand, **indirect costs** are less obvious. They represent the costs of infrastructure and daily business at your institution. For example, the books in the library are an indirect cost because, although you may use them for your project, everyone else in the institution can use them as well. The building where the tutors provide services is an indirect cost because, although the project tutors work there, there may also be several departments, classrooms, and a café in the building. In both of these examples, the books and the building are used for multiple purposes, so it is very difficult to quantify what portions of their cost should be attributed to the grant.

For universities, indirect costs include such items as the following:

- Computer equipment and software
- Utilities (electricity, water, garbage)
- Facilities maintenance (repairing the roof, maintaining the elevators, etc.)
- Information technology (IT) services
- Library resources and services
- Accounting
- Grants administration (compliance, stewardship, etc.)
- General supplies (pens, copy paper, print cartridges, staplers, etc.)
- And more!

For a full list see the A-21, which will be explained a little later.

Federal agencies recognize that indirect costs are a real part of grants. After all, grants would be much more difficult to pursue if universities did not have such a varied and flexible set of facilities and services already available. Federal agencies, therefore, often award indirect costs as part of a grant according to a percentage set individually for each institution, called the **indirect cost rate.**

For proposals to most federal funders, the indirect rate is included in the request. If the award maximum is $100,000 and your college or university has an indirect rate of 30% (which is fairly low), then $30,000 of the grant will go toward indirect costs. In real terms, this means that the direct cost request or the items that you put on your budget to run your project must total $70,000 for a $100,000 request.

One benefit of working at a predominantly undergraduate institution (PUI) is that the indirect rates are often lower. Research institutions may have indirect rates of 50 percent or more.

Federal Unallowable Costs

Although there are a great many federal documents that govern granting, the most useful one for the PI is the **A-21, Cost Principles for Educational Institutions**. It may not surprise you to know that there are different cost principles for hospitals, nonprofit organizations, for-profit organizations, and other institutions that commonly receive federal grant funding. The A-21 catalogs several **unallowable costs**, that is, expenses that federal grants will not pay (OMB, 2004). With experience, PIs get a sense of what can and cannot be included in a federal grant budget. To get started, you can find a general breakdown of the unallowable costs in Appendix 1 of this book. One rule of thumb is to keep in mind that federal grants are taxpayer money and therefore must be used for work-related activities. Nothing that seems remotely like fun (celebratory meals, alcohol, leisure pursuits, etc.) can be included, nor can expenses that the federal government considers the institution's responsibility or donations of any kind.

BUDGET NARRATIVES AND JUSTIFICATIONS

Budget narratives and **justifications** are two names for the same thing: a document that breaks down the lines of the budget, explaining exactly what is needed for the project and why. The budget justification is normally a Word document, possibly converted into a PDF file, formatted to match the general proposal narrative and organized along the same lines as the budget. The reviewer should easily be able to refer between the budget and the budget narrative in the review process.

The most extensive budget justifications require not only the purpose of each cost but also how it was estimated and its importance to the project. Some funders prefer that calculations be included in the budget narrative, and some do not. If instructions are not given clearly in the RFP, one way to figure out how much information should be included is to consider whether the budget justification has page limits. For example, the NSF budget justification is limited to three pages. This greatly reduces the amount of information that can be presented. Other agencies have no limits on the length of the budget justification, leading to more detail and longer documents.

Unfortunately, during the rush to complete a well-written narrative, the budget justification is often neglected. Yet the budget justification is an important opportunity to strengthen the narrative by explaining exactly why various resources are needed. This is particularly true for short, research-based narrative submissions. For example, at 15 pages the research-intensive NSF project description will often not allow for discussion of items of need, payment arrangements, or relevant details of costing, even when these need to be addressed directly. It is therefore very important to make the case for all budget line items, and particularly unusual items in the budget narrative. This is particularly true when an item requested falls outside the parameters of the funder's guidelines.

> ### Box 6.7   Budget Justifications Help the Proposal
>
> Although the production of a budget narrative requires extra work, it is worth the effort. The fact is, creating a budget justification requires that you go over every single line of the budget in detail, checking each item carefully. Errors tend to emerge when a budget narrative is done well—you will see things left out, things not summed up correctly, and things that should be deleted. Sometimes the errors are serious and can cause a great deal of trouble if left unattended, so a well-constructed budget justification pays off in the long run.

SUBAWARDS

Subawards are awards split between two or more collaborators who work at different colleges or universities. Each institution has a specific budget, created according to its own administrative and contextual needs; therefore, each subaward will have a different indirect cost rate, and grant employee pay rates will be costed out according to each institution's normal practice. When a project is subject to subawards, one institution will stand as the **prime** or responsible party for the entire award. The prime will receive the award from the funder and disperse it to the subawarded institutions according to the proposal budget.

Participating in larger projects by receiving a subaward is a great way for new PIs to begin their grant careers:

- Receiving a subaward is considered by many colleges and universities to be the same as receiving a grant award outright. Working on a subaward gives you the opportunity to learn how to run a large grant.
- Receiving a subaward allows you to do important work without the headache of serving as the lead PI.
- For PIs working at PUIs, receiving a subaward can allow the project to be more competitive, because the prime is usually the most prestigious research institution. In other words, the reviewers will think of the project as belonging to the prime, and when the prime is a research institution, this can help in terms of award consideration.

If you have the opportunity to participate in a subaward, take it. There will be a few differences in the submission, however. Keep the following in mind:

- **The prime will perform the submission,** so you will need to take direction from the lead PI and possibly her sponsored projects officers in creating materials to be added to the proposal.
- **You will need to keep your own sponsored projects office informed** about your participation in the submission. There may very well be paperwork involved, and doing all of that at the last minute may not work very well for your team.
- **Create your own budget** according to the rules of the submission and according to the prime's requirements, which may be a little different.
- **Your deadline will be due well before the main project deadline,** because your materials must be incorporated into the prime's submission.
- **You will need to negotiate your part of the request with the prime**. Expect the prime to take the larger part of the award.

WORKING WITH YOUR SPONSORED PROJECTS OFFICE

The budget is, hands down, the most interesting part of a grant for sponsored projects personnel. This is because of the sponsored projects office's responsibility for compliance, the importance of the budget for successful implementation of the project, and the reality of institutional liability. A significant part of any sponsored projects office mission is to ensure that the relevant rules are applied to each budget as well as the rest of the proposal and that all costable items in the narrative are included in the budget.

How the sponsored projects office expresses these concerns varies considerably between institutions. In some places, there is a central sponsored projects office that will check over the proposal before submission, particularly the budget, and send it back to the PI with commentary on changes that need to be made. Some universities with strong central sponsored projects offices will have departmental-level personnel to assist PIs with hands-on budget work, and this is a significant form of assistance. Although a PUI may produce a relatively low volume of grants, it may have a central office that offers a great deal of hands-on help in addition to checking budgets for compliance.

In any case, it behooves the PI to understand and embrace the budgeting process—even if only to be sure that the budget reflects his understanding of the project—and to be able to communicate effectively with sponsored projects personnel.

THE NUTS & BOLTS

1. A budget is a list of expenses that reflects the needs for the project, the types of costs the funder is willing to provide, and the way the college or university does business.

2. The budget should include all required expenses and be costed out accurately, to the best knowledge of the PI.

3. If the grant includes match or cost share, ascertain very early whether and how your institution will provide this.

4. When estimating a budget line, do not forget to include ancillary expenses like shipping, taxes, and fees.

5. Know your institution's indirect cost rate and how this affects your budget.

EXERCISES: WORKING TOWARD MASTERY

Create a budget based on your logic model from Chapter 5. Use the resources column from your logic model to begin the budget: You can copy the resources column directly into a spreadsheet program and begin costing each line out. Follow the specific guidance offered in this chapter and Case Study 2: Preparing a Federal Budget. If you do not have a funder in mind, use the budget organization given in this chapter.

CHAPTER TERMS

A-21, Cost Principles for Educational Institutions: A federal document that sets out the appropriate principles for estimating a federally funded budget for colleges and universities.

Budget narrative or justification: A document submitted on request of the funder that presents all the details of how the budget total was arrived at, including estimates for item costs, shipping, taxes, and fees as well as the purpose for each item in the project (see Case Study 3 for detail on creating a budget narrative).

Cost out: The process of estimating the cost of each item in a budget, including the per unit expense, the number of units, tax, shipping, installation, and so forth.

Direct costs: Items from a budget that directly fund project activities and can be discreetly identified.

Indirect costs: Usually a percentage of the direct costs of the budget added on to the total, estimated to represent the services and facilities provided to the project by the university that cannot easily be enumerated or measured. Examples of indirect costs include electricity, facilities, and library services.

Match (cost sharing): Funds, goods, or services provided by an organization, in addition to grant funding, to help support a project.

Meals and incidental expenses (M&IE): Sustenance and necessary expenses incurred while traveling. M&IE is an alternative to per diem and is paid according to receipts received.

Overhead (administrative costs): A term often used to refer to indirect costs when charged to a foundation. Overhead is often set by foundations at a specific rate of, for example, 10 percent, 12 percent, or 15 percent.

Prime: The lead institution in a subawarded grant. The prime is responsible for the project and supervises the partner institution's efforts according to federal principles.

Request: The total amount of money requested in a grant proposal.

Subaward: The portion of the budget intended to fund a part of a project occurring at another organization. The subaward is budgeted according to the practice and under the supervision of the prime or receiving institution as well as on the basis of federal principles.

Unallowable costs: In federal budgets, costs which the federal government will not fund toward a grant project. Unallowable costs are discussed in Appendix 1.

CASE STUDY 2

Preparing a Federal Budget

INTRODUCTION

This case study will detail the preparation of a budget for the National Science Foundation (NSF) as an example of the concepts presented in Chapter 5. This case study is designed to answer a good many (although perhaps not all) questions of those PIs without access to budget assistance from a sponsored project office.

Please note that this budget has been developed to provide a wide range of examples, demonstrating lines that might be found in a social science proposal. It has NOT been developed as a proposal budget for submission. It is important to keep in mind that the NSF has extensive and useful guidance for the creation of budgets. NSF proposers should work closely with both the latest version of the Grant Proposal Guide (GPG) and with FastLane help files. You can find the GPG on the NSF website (www.nsf.gov): search "GPG." To find the FastLane help files, navigate to FastLane from the NSF website (there is a link on the homepage) and then click the help link. These are the authoritative sources on NSF grant submissions.

Using Spreadsheet Software

Before we begin to break this budget down into component parts, we will go over some simple versions of the calculations to be used in the spreadsheet software to prepare it.

Cost entries will be referred to by the cell they appear in. Lines with calculations have been numbered and columns, lettered, as below.

The equation will appear next to the cell, with an explanation under it.

Figure CS2.1   Labeling Cells

Note the shaded cell, G10. This is how we will refer to cells in the example budget.

Example calculation:

$$G10 = (E10/9) * F10^1$$

Total Year 1 grant salary = the total annual institutional salary ÷ nine months × the number of months requested (with salaries appearing in Column E and months requested appearing in Column F).

It is customary in multiyear grants to build rises each year of 2 or 3 percent to account for cost-of-living increases to employee salaries when the institution awards these. Year 2 salaries therefore will be calculated as follows:

$$H10 = G10 * 1.02^2$$

Year 2 effort (2 months summer stipend) = Year 1 effort + 2%.

All line totals across the two project years will be calculated as follows:

$$I10 = G10 + H10$$

Total line = Year 1 total + Year 2 total.

---

[1] * means "to multiply by" in many software programs. It will be given in cell calculations, while × will be used in explanations.

[2] .02 or 2 percent represents a year-to-year cost-of-living increase. Check with your sponsored projects office regarding university policy on this.

COMPLETE EXAMPLE BUDGET

Bob Miller, a sociologist interested in STEM education, is proposing a project to examine how STEM subjects are taught at the university level. He will submit the proposal to the Research and Evaluation on Education in Science and Engineering (REESE) Program of the NSF. The deadline is July 17, 2012, at 5pm local time, and the program solicitation is NSF 12–552.[3]

Since he has already performed a pilot study on the intervention and he has two partner universities, Dr. Miller will propose a medium empirical project, which awards up to $1.5 million over three years.

First Dr. Miller will set up an internal budget using a two-year template. When the proposal is complete, he will copy the relevant figures into the NSF form, which is located in the NSF online submission portal, FastLane.

The main budget sections for the NSF include the following:

- Senior personnel
- Other personnel
- Fringe benefits
- Equipment
- Travel
- Participant support costs
- Other direct costs

Dr. Miller will set the budget up with a totals area that includes the following:

- Direct costs
- Modified total direct costs (MTDC)
- Facilities & administration (F&A or indirect costs)[4]
- Total request

The complete budget appears below.

The budget includes areas where figures are given for specific aspects of the equations. Because of space limitations, I have not always included a separate cell for each part of the equation; however, all of the information is in the line description and in the cell calculation. This reflects the way I actually do budgets. Of course, there are other ways to do a budget, and I have seen many correct versions of this sort of table. Feel free to set your budget up according to your own style; just be sure that you have provided all the information required and that you calculate it correctly!

---

[3]As of August 2012, all of this information was current; however, like any funding agency, the NSF does change programs and deadlines. Readers interested in REESE should read the latest information from the NSF website. Search "REESE."

[4]F&A is a very common term for indirect costs and often appears in federal budget forms.

Figure CS2.2 Complete Example NSF Budget

A	B	C	D	E	F	G	H	I
1			Working (Internal) Budget					
2			**Bob Miller, Sociology**					
3			Teaching STEM Subjects in Introductory University Courses (TSUIC)					
4			NSF REESE					
5			Deadline: July 17					
6								
7			*Item*			*6/1/2013– 5/31/2014*	*6/1/2014– 5/31/2015*	*Total*
8			**1. Senior Personnel (All Salaries Subject to 2% Rise Per Year)**					
9			A. Bob Miller, PI, 2 months summer effort	$82,440	2	$18,320	$18,686	$37,006
10			B. Mahmud Jamal, co-PI, 15% effort (1 course remission per year)	$76,780	.15	$11,517	$11,747	$23,264
11			C. Mahmud Jamal, co-PI, 1 month summer effort	$76,780	1	$8,531	$8,702	$17,233

(Continued)

A	B	C	D	E	F	G	H	I
12			D. Chandra Simms, statistician, 2 weeks summer effort	$95,101	.5	$5,283	$5,389	$10,672
13			**Subtotal Senior Personnel**			**$43,652**	**$44,525**	**$88,176**
14								
15			**2. Other Personnel**					
16			E. TBD, project coordinator, 50% effort, 12 months	$45,000	.5	$22,500	$22,950	$45,450
17			F. TBD 2 graduate assistants, 20 hours × 36 weeks × $18	18	2	$25,920	$26,438	$52,358
18			**Subtotal MTDC, Other Personnel**			**$48,420**	**$49,388**	**$97,808**
19			G. TBD 2 graduate assistants, annual tuition, $4,581 × 3 quarters × 2 students	$13,743	2	$27,486	$28,860	$56,346
20			**Subtotal Non-MTDC Other Personnel**			**$27,486**	**$28,860**	**$56,346**
21			**Subtotal Other Personnel**			**$75,906**	**$78,249**	**$154,155**
22								
23			**Subtotal Salaries and Wages**			**$119,558**	**$122,773**	**$242,331**
24								

A	B	C	D	E	F	G	H	I
25			3. Fringe Benefits					
26			A. Fringe charged to employees at federal rate (32.3%)			$21,367	$21,794	$43,161
27			B. Fringe charged at student rate (4.5%) on student wages only			$1,166	$1,190	$2,356
28			C. Fringe charged at student rate (4.5%) on graduate tuition only			$1,237	$1,299	$2,536
29			Subtotal Fringe			$23,770	$24,283	$48,053
30			Total Personnel			$143,328	$147,056	$290,384
31								
32			4. Equipment					
33			Not applicable					
34								
35			5. Travel					
36			Domestic Travel					
37			A. PI to Washington, D.C., for REESE annual meeting					
38			i. Round-trip airfare (Expedia. com) to Washington, D.C.	$600	1	$600	$600	$1,200

(Continued)

Figure CS2.2 (Continued)

A	B	C	D	E	F	G	H	I
39			ii. Lodging (GSA) $183 × 2 days	$183	2		$366	$732
40			iii. MI&E, $71 (GSA) × 3 days	$71	3	$213	$213	$426
41			B. Project leadership team (2) presents at 1 conference per year (Y1 domestic, Y2 foreign)					
42			*American Educational Research Association (AERA) 2013 in San Francisco, April 27–May 1, 2013*					
43			iv. Round-trip airfare (Expedia. com) $300 × 2 individuals	$300	2	$600		$600
44			v. Lodging (U.S. General Services Administration) $155 × 5 nights × 2 individuals	$155	5	$1,550		$1,550
45			vi. M&IE (U.S. General Services Administration) $71 × 6 days × 2 individuals	$71	6	$852		$852
46			vii. Conference fees (AE) $300 × 2 individuals	$300	2	$600		$600
47			C. Mileage: Graduate assistants' mileage to school sites. University to site 1: 45 miles; university to site 2: 26 miles; university to site 3: 13 miles; 6 trips per year. 83 miles × 6 trips × 2 grad students × .555	0.555	83	$553	$553	$1,106

A	B	C	D	E	F	G	H	I
48			**Subtotal Domestic Travel**			$5,334	$1,732	$7,066
49			**Foreign Travel**					
50			D. Project leadership team (2) presents at 1 conference per year (Y1 domestic, Y2 foreign)					
51			*International Educators' Conference, September 2014, Stockholm*					
52			i. Round-trip airfare (Expedia. com) $1,900 × 2 individuals	$1,900	2	$0	$3,800	$3,800
53			ii. Lodging (U.S. General Services Administration) $268 × 3 nights	$268	3	$0	$1,608	$1,608
54			iii. MI&E (U.S. General Services Administration) $150 × 5 days	$150	5	$0	$1,500	$1,500
55			iv. Conference fees (AE) $300 × 2 individuals	$300	2	$0	$600	$600
56			**Subtotal Foreign Travel**			$0	$7,508	$7,508
57			**Subtotal Travel**			$5,334	$9,240	$14,574
58								
59		**6. Participant Support Costs**						
60			A. Participant (faculty) conference					

(Continued)

Figure CS2.2 (Continued)

A	B	C	D	E	F	G	H	I
61			i. Sustenance for one 6-hour local participant conference; 75 box lunches × $8.50	$8.50	75	$638	$638	$1,275
62			ii. Light beverage service	$150	1	$150	$150	$300
63			B. Participant incentives, 30 random student interviews (15 experiments + 15 control = 30 students × $25) each year	$25	30	$750	$750	$1,500
64			**Subtotal Participant Support Costs**			**$1,538**	**$1,538**	**$3,075**
65								
66			**7. Other Direct Costs**					
67			*Materials and Supplies*					
68			A. Program handbooks for each conference participant, printed by campus graphics (250 pages × .05) + $1.55 three-ring binders × 75 participants	$250	75	$1,054	$1,054	$2,108
69			B. 4 iPads: 2 MC770LL/A tablet (32GB, Wi-Fi, black) 14 × $525 × 8.25%	$525	4	$2,273		$2,273
70			**Subtotal Materials and Supplies**			**$3,327**	**$1,054**	**$4,381**

A	B	C	D	E	F	G	H	I
71								
72			*Consultant Services*					
73			i. Hsieh Da-Xia 10 days × $450	$450	10	$4,500	$4,500	$9,000
74			ii. Tom Murray 10 days × $550	$550	10	$5,500	$5,500	$11,000
75			iii. Françoise Albert × $650	$650	10	$6,500	$6,500	$13,000
76			**Subtotal Consultant Services**			**$16,500**	**$16,500**	**$33,000**
77								
78			*Subcontracts*					
79			i. Alex Gonzalez, Small Liberal Arts College			$105,980	$110,239	$216,219
80			ii. Linda Johnson, Large Public University			$106,000	$109,456	$215,456
81			**Subtotal Subcontracts**			**$211,980**	**$219,695**	**$431,675**
82								
83			**Subtotal Other Direct Costs**			$231,807	$237,249	**$469,056**
84								

(Continued)

119

Figure CS2.2 (Continued)

A	B	C	D	E	F	G	H	I
85			**8. Total Direct Costs**			$382,006	$395,082	$777,088
86			**9. Modified Total Direct Costs (MTDC)**			$189,766	$143,690	$333,456
87			**10. Facilities & Administrative Costs (F&A) at 48%**			$91,087	$68,971	$160,059
88								
89			**11. Total Request**			**$473,093**	**$464,053**	**$937,147**

For the most part, we will be estimating Year 1 expenses and so will be dealing with Column G. When we are dealing with Year 2 expenses, we will use Column H. Column I represents total expenses for the project (Year 1 or Column G + Year 2 or Column H) by line.

1. Senior Personnel

Line 9, A. Bob Miller, PI, is listed first and is requesting two months summer effort for this project. This request is in line with standard NSF budgeting policy, which restricts faculty members to two months salary per year, often taken as a summer stipend.

$$G9 = (E9/9) * F9$$

Year 1 effort = total annual salary/9 months × 2 months effort.

Line 10, B. Mahmud Jamal, co-PI, is listed next, and he is requesting one course remission per year for the two years of this project. One course remission is costed at 15% of his annual salary per university guidelines.

$$G10 = E10 * F10$$

Year 1 effort (one course remission) = annual salary ×15% effort.

Line 11, C. Mahmud Jamal, co-PI, requests summer support.

Line 12, D. Chandra Simms, statistician and collaborator, is requesting two weeks of summer effort. Two weeks will be represented as .5, equaling one half of a one-month effort.

$$G12 = (E12/9) * .5$$

Year 1 effort (2 weeks summer stipend) = annual salary/9 months × 2 weeks effort.

Line 13, Subtotal Senior Personnel

$$G13 = G9 + G10 + G11 + G12$$

$$H13 = H9 + H10 + H11 + H12$$

$$I13 = G13 + H13$$

2. Other Personnel

Line 16, E. TBD, project coordinator, is unnamed because he is not yet employed by the university. This position will work 50% time (or .5 FTE, 20 hours per week) for 12 months per year as a staff member. The PI has submitted the job description and is citing the salary estimate provided by his sponsored projects office.

$$G16 = E16 * F16$$

Year 1 effort = annual salary × .5 FTE.

Line 17, F. Two graduate student assistants will work for $18 per hour, 20 hours per week, 36 weeks per year on the project. They will also receive full tuition.

$$G17 = E17 * 20 * 36 * F17$$

Year 1 effort = $18 × 20 hours × 36 weeks × 2 students.

Line 18, Subtotal MTDC,[5] Other Personnel Costs

$$G18 = G16 + G17$$

Subtotal MTDC other personnel salary cost = the salary for the project coordinator + the wages of the two graduate RAs.

Line 19, G. Tuition for two graduate assistants. Many research universities work tuition into the grant as part of graduate student support packages. Tuition is not covered in MTDC, so it is a good idea to separate it out somehow in the budget.

$$G19 = E19 * F19$$

Year 1 effort = estimated annual tuition × 2 students.

$$H19 = G19 * 1.05$$

Year 2 effort = Year 1 annual tuition + 5%.

Tuition rises at widely different rates at different institutions, and from one year to the next. Five percent is estimated here for Year 2.

Line 20, Subtotal Non-MTDC Other Personnel Costs. These will be left out of the MTDC total.

Line 21, Subtotal Other Personnel Costs. These include all other (nonsenior) personnel.

$$G21 = G18 + G20$$

Line 23, Subtotal Salaries and Wages = the subtotal of MTDC other personnel costs + non-MTDC other personnel costs.

3. Fringe Benefits

Fringe benefits are represented in the budget as a percentage rate multiplied by wages and salaries in order to pay for health insurance, disability insurance, worker's compensation, unemployment insurance, and so forth. When an institution negotiates an indirect cost rate with a federal agency, a federal fringe rate is usually assigned and will typically be different from the institution's own base fringe rate. Institutions with negotiated federal fringe rates must charge these on all federal grants.

---

[5]MTDC or modified total direct costs is a rather complex topic having to do with the appropriate charging of direct and indirect costs. Your sponsored projects office will probably handle estimating it. If you must estimate MTDC yourself, you will find more information at the end of this budget in line 85.

Line 26, A. Fringe charged to employees at the institution's federal rate. Fringe is charged here to employees (faculty and staff) at the federal rate (32.3%).

$$G26 = (G13 + G16) * .323$$

Year 1 faculty and staff fringe = the salary cost of Bob Miller, Mahmud Jamal, Chandra Simms, and the TBD program coordinator × 32.3%.

Line 27, B. Fringe charged at student rate (4.5%) for student wages. This line includes only student hourly compensation, multiplied by the student fringe rate of 4.5%.

$$G27 = G17 * .045$$

Year 1 student fringe = the cost of the student wages × 4.5%.

Line 28, C. Fringe charged at student rate (4.5%) for graduate student tuition—this line is separated out because training costs cannot be included in MTDC.

$$G28 = G19 * .045$$

Year 1 student fringe = cost of student tuition × 4.5%.

Line 29, Subtotal Fringe, totals up all fringe costs.

$$G29 = G26 + G27 + G28$$

Line 30, Total Personnel, includes all personnel expenses for team members employed at the prime university.

$$G30 = G23 + G29$$

Year 1 total personnel costs = the total cost of salaries and wages + the total cost of fringe benefits for Year 1.

4. Equipment

Not applicable for this project.

5. Travel

Domestic travel: We break out domestic and foreign travel per NSF guidelines.

A. PI to Washington, D.C., to attend REESE annual meeting

Line 38, A.i. Round-trip airfare is the actual rate on Expedia as of publication, which was about $533. This does not include the $50 baggage fees ($25 each way) and taxes, which brings the estimated total to about $600.

$$G38 = E38 * F38$$

The total airfare = estimated cost of round-trip flight × the number of individuals (PI).

Line 39, A.ii. Lodging. E38 is the daily cost of lodging as offered by the U.S. General Services Administration (GSA).[6] F39 is the number of nights.

$$G39 = E39 * F39 * 1$$

Year 1 lodging = the per-night GSA estimation of the cost of a room × the number of nights × the number of individuals traveling.

Line 40, A.iii. M&IE, is also estimated using the GSA. Some universities have standard M&IE rates, so it is a good idea to check before budgeting the GSA M&IE. Federal funds may not be used to purchase alcohol, even as part of M&IE.

$$G40 = E40 * F40 * 1$$

Year 1 M&IE = per-day GSA estimate of expenses × the number of days × the number of individuals.

Next the project leadership team (PI and co-PI) were scheduled to present at the American Educational Research Association (AERA) conference as part of the dissemination plan. AERA was held in San Francisco in 2013 (lines 42–46). Airfare, lodging, and M&IE are budgeted in the same way as in the previous event. Conference fees are taken from the organizational website.

Line 47, C. Mileage, reimburses mileage for graduate RAs as they travel from school to school doing data collection. Mileage can be paid for projects that require driving above and beyond normal car use. Use the mileage rate found on the IRS website (www.irs.gov). Search for "standard mileage rate." You will get a figure in cents (.51, .56, etc.). This is how much should be paid per mile to reimburse for gas and wear and tear on the automobile. Estimate mileage using a mapping program or website.

$$G47 = E47 * F47 * 6 * 2$$

Total Year 1 mileage = the IRS reimbursement rate × number of miles × number of trips × number of individuals.

---

[6]Find these rates by searching "per diem" on the GSA website (www.gsa.gov). Although it is called per diem, we will handle it as M&IE.

Line 48, Subtotal Domestic Travel. The NSF will require domestic travel as one line, so we subtotal here.

$$G48 = G38 + G39 + G40 + G43 +$$
$$G44 + G45 + G46 + G47$$

The total Year 1 cost of domestic travel equals all domestic travel lines summed up.

Foreign Travel

Because the foreign trip will take place in Year 2, we will cost out Column H for this section rather than G.

Line 52, D.i. Round-trip airfare. The actual rates on Expedia to Stockholm as of publication ranged from $1,745 to $1,829, which was rounded up to $1,900 to accommodate baggage costs and other fees in both directions.

$$H52 = E52 * F52$$

The total airfare for Year 2 = estimated cost of round-trip flight × the number of individuals (PI and co-PI).

Line 53, D.ii. Lodging. The lodging rate is taken from the Department of State pages.[7]

$$H53 = E53 * F53 * 2$$

The total cost of lodging for Year 2 = the State estimate of nightly lodging for Stockholm × the number of nights × the number of individuals (PI and co-PI).

Line 54, D.iii. M&IE. With long flights, it is wise to schedule one or two travel days in addition to the estimated visit days. Foreign M&IE is also taken from the U.S. Department of State website.

$$H54 = E54 * F54 * 2$$

The total cost of M&IE for Year 2 = State estimate of M&IE costs for Stockholm × the number of days × the number of individuals (PI and co-PI).

Line 55, D.iv. Conference Fees. Acquire these costs from the organization website.

$$H55 = E55 * F55$$

Year 2 conference fees = the cost of the conference × number of individuals.

---

[7]Go to the U.S. Department of State pages (www.state.gov) and search "foreign per diem rates." Again, although these are given as per diem, we will handle them as M&IE.

Line 56, Foreign Travel Subtotal

$$H56 = H52 + H53 + H54 + H55 \text{ or Sum}(H52:H55)$$

Total foreign travel for Year 2 = total of all foreign airfare, lodging, M&IE, and conference fees.

Line 57, subtotal travel includes both domestic and foreign subtotals.

$$H57 = H48 + H56$$

Subtotal travel = subtotal domestic travel + subtotal foreign travel.

6. Participant Support

Line 61, A.i. Sustenance for the participant conference. When budgeting for an event with hospitality, consider not only the cost of food but also drinks, the service, tableware, tables and other furniture, the venue, and possibly costs of cleanup. Ask whether these items are included in the caterer's foodservice quote.

$$G61 = E61 * F61$$

Total cost of meals = cost per item × number of meals.

Line 62, A.ii. Light beverage service. Be sure to check on whether beverages are provided with the meals or whether this is an additional cost.

$$G62 = E62 * F62$$

Total beverage service = total cost of beverage service × number of days beverage service requested.

Line 63, B. Participant incentives provides funds to pay participants a small sum for taking part in the research. Because this is not a requirement for the class they are taking and because the interview is estimated to last at least 90 minutes, each interviewee will be offered $25.

Payments will be offered in the form of gift cards that the participants will be required to sign for at the university cashier's office. Each participant will receive $25 to participate in the initial interview.

$$G63 = E63 * F63$$

The total cost of Year 1 participant incentives = the amount of payment × the number of participants.

Line 64, Subtotal Participant Support Costs. These costs will not be included in the MTDC.

$$G64 = G61 + G62 + G63$$

Total participant costs support = conference meals + conference beverage service + participant incentives.

7. Other Direct Costs

The other direct costs area of an NSF budget includes everything else. The first subcategory here is materials and supplies.

Materials and supplies

As noted in Chapter 5, materials and supplies can present some challenges. Items included in this section should be identifiable and not considered part of F&A or indirect costs.

Line 68, A. Program handbooks for each conference. If this item is sent out to a print shop and is invoiced separately, it can be included in the budget. When budgeting for print jobs, be sure to consider the costs of binding and tax, which, in this case, is included in the per item cost.

$$G68 = [(E68 * 0.05) + 1.55] * F68$$

The Year 1 total cost of conference handbooks = [(the number of pages × cost per page) + cost of one three-ring binder] x the number of handbooks.

Line 69, B. iPads for data collection purposes. The PI has researched the cost online and sees that iPad models cost between $450 and $599. He chooses the average price to be sure he can purchase the items and keeps a copy of the estimate in his files.

Even though the PI intends to order these items online, sales tax may still be applied, depending on state law. Shipping may be free; however, this must be ascertained carefully, particularly for large items. Forgetting to check on shipping costs can result in unplanned charges to the grant.

$$G69 = E69 * F69 * 1.0825$$

Total price of the iPads in Year 1 = estimated price per iPad × number of iPads × tax.

Line 70, Subtotal Materials and Supplies

$$G70 = G68 + G69$$

Year 1 subtotal of materials and supplies = the estimated cost of program handbooks for participants + the cost of iPads for student participants.

Consultant Services

Consultants generally charge an hourly or daily rate for their services. Some federal agencies have a "consultant rate" that should be budgeted; for example, the Office of Justice Programs once limited consultants to $450 per day (and may still do so). High consultant fees need to be carefully justified in the budget narrative.

In this case, three educational consultants will be retained for two weeks (10 working days) over the summer to provide feedback on project progress. NSF does not have a standard consultant rate, so each consultant has provided his or her customary price, which will be discussed in the budget narrative. Hsieh Da-Xia is local and so will not have to travel to join the project meeting; however, Tom Murray and Françoise Albert are both located at a distance, and their travel expenses have been added to their daily rate estimates. It is also possible to include the costs of consultant travel in separate lines.

All consultant lines are costed out as follows:

$$G73 = E73 * F73$$

$$G74 = E74 * F74$$

$$G75 = E75 * F75$$

The total consultant cost for each year = the daily rate × the number of days.

Line 76, Subtotal Consultant Services

$$I76 = G76 + H76$$

Subcontracts

Subcontracts refer to subordinate budgets that will be implemented at other institutions. Each institution has a local budget page in the prime's budget spreadsheet. When adding the total to these cells, you would follow the same equation steps; however, you would select the total of the specific subaward spreadsheet for inclusion here.

$$G79 = SLAC!F72^{[8]}$$

Total Year 1 costs from Small Liberal Arts College (SLAC) worksheet.

$$G80 = LPU!G72^{[9]}$$

Total Year 1 costs from Large Public University (LPU) worksheet.

Each subsequent year would include the total cell from the subcontract spreadsheet. The total Year 1 subcontract line is calculated by adding the total Year 1 expenses of Small Liberal Arts College and Large Public University.

Line 81, Subtotal Subcontracts

$$G81 = G79 + G80$$

---

[8]This code, specific to Excel, indicates that this figure is imported from spreadsheet SLAC, where the figures for Small Liberal Arts College are located.

[9]This code, specific to Excel, indicates that this figure is imported from spreadsheet LPU, where figures for Large Public University are located.

Line 83, Subtotal Other Direct Costs
Use each previous subtotal in the section.

$$G83 = G70 + G76 + G81$$

Indirect Costs or F&A

For most PIs, the sponsored projects office will provide information on totaling up indirect costs. For now what is important to keep in mind is that some items from the budget cannot be included in the calculation of indirect costs. In the case of this budget, the following items will not be included: graduate assistant tuition (Line 19) and fringe on tuition (Line 28), participant support costs (Lines 61–64), and all costs of the subcontracts over $25,000 each (Lines 79–80).

Totaling the Budget

Just as there are several ways to create a budget, there are several ways to total one. This simple example will serve to demonstrate the main points involved.

Line 85, Total Direct Costs, should include all the costs of the project, and in this example, all the subtotals of the budget.

$$G85 = G30 + G57 + G64 + G83$$

Total direct costs = subtotal personnel + subtotal travel + subtotal participant support + subtotal other direct costs.

Line 86, modified total direct costs (MTDC)

$$G86 = G13 + G18 + G26 + G27 + G57 + G70 + G76 + \$25{,}000 + \$25{,}000$$

MTDC = the costs of senior personnel + other personnel (excluding tuition) + fringe benefits of senior personnel + fringe benefits of other personnel (excluding those based on tuition) + travel + materials and supplies + the total cost of the consultant lines + $25,000 for each of the two subcontracts. (Subcontract maximum is $25,000 per institution for the entire grant.)

Line 87, Facilities & Administrative (F&A or Indirect) Costs. To estimate the F&A line of the proposal, multiply the MTDC by the indirect cost rate of the university.

$$G87 = G86 * .48$$

Line 89, Total Request, is calculated by adding the total direct costs line to the indirect line.

$$G89 = G85 + G87$$

CASE STUDY 3

Creating a Budget Justification or Narrative

INTRODUCTION

The following example budget justification is a thorough rendition of the budget given in Case Study 2. This document was written without consideration of page limits, so please keep in mind that if you ever actually apply to the National Science Foundation (NSF), the budget narrative will be limited to three pages.

EXAMPLE BUDGET JUSTIFICATION

U.S. Department of Education

Robert Miller, sociology

"Teaching STEM Subjects in Introductory University Courses"

Budget Justification

All salaries subject to 2% annual rise.

1. Senior Personnel

A. Robert Miller, PhD, PI: 2 months annual summer effort

    Dr. Miller (full professor of sociology) will lead the project, design the interventions, supervise all personnel and the research process at all levels—including training for project personnel on data gathering and input, random spot data checks, risk management, and guidance on statistical analysis. Dr. Miller will write up results for publication.

$$Y1\ \$18{,}320 + Y2\ \$18{,}686 = \$37{,}006$$

B. Mahmud Jamal, PhD, co-PI: 1 course remission annually (15% effort)

C. Mahmud Jamal, PhD, co-PI: 1 month summer effort

Dr. Jamal (assistant professor of sociology) will conduct interventions and directly supervise the project coordinator and graduate students. Dr. Jamal will closely monitor video recording of teaching sessions and coding of tapes by graduate student assistants and will assist in the write-up of results for publication. One course remission is requested per year because of his heavy teaching load (3–3).

$$\text{Course remission: }Y1\ \$11{,}517 + Y2\ \$11{,}747 = \$23{,}264$$

$$\text{Summer stipend: }Y1\ \$8{,}531 + Y2\ \$8{,}702 = \$17{,}233$$

D. Chandra Simms, PhD, statistician: 2 weeks annual summer effort

Dr. Simms, associate professor of mathematics, will provide statistical analysis for the project.

$$Y1\ \$5{,}283 + Y2\ \$5{,}389 = \$10{,}672$$

2. Other Personnel

E. Project coordinator—TBD: 50% effort, 12 months

The project coordinator will be a BA- or MA-level employee charged with implementing the data-gathering plan under the supervision of Dr. Miller and Dr. Jamal. This will include scheduling videotaping sessions with faculty, ensuring that video equipment is set up for sessions, and supervising coding sessions between the graduate students. The project coordinator will track each tape through the data-gathering and analysis process, assuring confidentiality and that the plan is implemented appropriately. The project coordinator will be available to assist with day-to-day questions about the project and will oversee the budget, interacting with various university offices as necessary.

$$Y1\ \$22{,}500 + Y2\ \$22{,}950 = \$45{,}450$$

F. Two graduate assistants, TBD: 2 students × 20 hours × 36 weeks × $18.

Two graduate students will be trained to code videotaped teaching sessions, thereby creating inter-rater reliability. Students will also prepare data for analysis and assist with setting up video equipment in classrooms.

Y1 $25,920 + Y2 $26,438 = $52,358

G. Graduate student tuition: $4,581 × 3 quarters × 2 students.

Tuition costs will be covered for the two graduate student RAs. Graduate tuition at the university is estimated to rise each year by 5 percent according to the graduate division.

Y1 $27,486 + Y2 $28,860 = $56,346

3. Fringe Benefits

The university has negotiated a fringe benefit rate of 32.3 percent for employees and 4.5 percent for students with Walter Smith (800–555–0199) of the Department of Health and Human Services (DHHS).[10] This rate will last until August 1, 2015.

A. **Fringe charged to employees:** Y1 $21,367 + Y2 $21,794 = $43,161.

B. **Fringe charged to student wages:** Y1 $1,166 + Y2 $1,190 = $2,356.

C. **Fringe charged to student tuition:** Y1 $1,237 + Y2 $1,299 = $2,536.

4. Equipment

Not applicable.

5. Travel

PI will attend annual REESE conference in Washington, D.C. Additionally, as part of the dissemination plan, the PI and co-PI will present at one conference per year. Year 1 will be at the AERA national conference and Year 2, the International Educators' Conference in Stockholm. The PI customarily presents every other year at the IE Conference as part of his ongoing international commitments. Please see PI's biosketch for details.

---

[10]This is a fictional person. Your assigned administrator will be listed on your university's F&A agreement.

A. **PI to Washington, D.C., for annual REESE Conference**

   i. **Round-trip airfare** (Expedia.com) to Washington, D.C.: $600 × 1 person = $600.

   ii. **Lodging** U.S. General Services Administration (GSA): $183 × 2 days × 1 person = $366.

   iii. **Meals and incidental expenses (M&IE)** (GSA): $71 × 3 days × 1 person = $213.

B. **PI and co-PI present at American Education Research Association (AERA),** April 2013, San Francisco.

   i. **Round-trip airfare** (Expedia.com) Los Angeles to San Francisco: $300 × 2 individuals = $600.

   ii. **Lodging,** San Francisco (GSA): $155 × 5 nights × 2 individuals = $1,550.

   iii. **M&IE** (GSA): $71 × 6 days × 2 individuals = $852.

   iv. **Conference fees:** $300 × 2 individuals = $600.

C. **Mileage:** graduate assistants; mileage to HEI sites.

   Graduate students will travel to three local university sites each year to gather data.

   University to Site 1 = 45 miles; University to Site 2 = 26 miles; University to Site 3 = 13 miles: 6 trips per year. 83 miles × 6 trips × 2 grad students × .555 = $553.

D. PI and co-PI present at **International Educators' Conference,** September 2014, Stockholm.

   i. **Round-trip airfare** (Expedia.com) Los Angeles to Stockholm: $1,900 × 2 individuals = $3,800.

   ii. **Lodging,** in Stockholm (State): $268 × 3 nights × 2 individuals = $1,608.

   iii. **M&IE** (State): $150 × 5 days × 2 individuals = $1,500.

   iv. **Conference Fees** (AE): $300 × 2 individuals = $600.

6. Participant Support Costs

The project will sponsor a yearly conference of participating faculty to present findings, gather participant impressions, and solidify research conclusions. Two of five sessions will be presented by participating faculty each year.

A. **Sustenance for participants** of one 6-hour local participant conference per year. 75 box lunches × $8.50 (cost per University Catering) = $638.

B. **Light beverage service** for one 6-hour local participant conference per year (cost per University Catering) = $150.

C. **Participant incentives:** Each year 30 students will be randomly invited to participate in one-on-one interviews to explore the nature of their classroom experience. Fifteen students will be randomly selected from study classrooms, and 15 will be randomly selected from control classrooms in the same subject. Students who complete the interview will receive a $25 incentive: 30 students × $25 = $750.

7. Other Direct Costs

Materials and Supplies

i. **Program Handbooks:** created for each conference participant, providing presentation materials from each speaker. Program handbooks will furnish participants with continuing access to the professional development provided at the annual conference. Printed by campus graphics. [(250 pages x .05) + $1.55 per three-ring binder] × 75 participants = $1,054.

ii. **Four iPads** for program personnel to collect data: These devices will be light and easy to use in the field. They will not be on the network in order to maintain privacy. Each device will be dedicated solely to project use. 4 iPads: MC770LL/A Tablet (32GB, Wi-Fi, Black) × $525 × 8.25% = $2,273.

Consultant Services

Three experienced educational consultants will be invited to participate in analysis of data gathered each summer and to attend the annual participant conference.

i. **Hsieh Da-Xia (expert, higher education science curriculum)** 10 days × $450 = $4,500 per year.

ii. **Tom Murray (expert, at-risk postsecondary students)** 10 days × $550 = $5,500 per year.

iii. **Françoise Albert (expert, higher education pedagogy)** 10 days × $650 = $6,500 per year.

Subcontracts

Collaborators from two other universities (Small Liberal Arts College and Large Public University) will replicate the project on a smaller scale at their institutions. Please see specific budget justifications for each school.

i. **Alex Gonzalez, Small Liberal Arts College**

Y1 $105,980 + Y2 $110,239 = $216,219

ii. **Linda Johnson, Large Public University**

Y1 $106,000 + Y2 $109,456 = $215,456

The University has negotiated an F&A (indirect) rate of 48 percent with Walter Smith (800–555–0199) of the Department of Health and Human Services (DHHS). This rate will last until August 1, 2015.[11]

---

[11]This is a fictional person. Consult the F&A agreement for your institution to discover your F&A administrator.

7

Traditional Letters of Interest and Proposals

INTRODUCTION

Now that you have a great idea, have developed a logic model, and have begun your budget, it is time to begin writing. For some people this is the fun part, and for others it is the hardest task associated with preparing grant proposals.

Writing is actually a very individual and even personal process: It is one way we present our view of the world to other people. Some people can write all day and produce pages of material, whereas others struggle to get started. Some people produce a great volume of text with little meaning, and others produce small amounts that are very dense and meaningful. All kinds of writers can be successful grant writers; the key is to be flexible, responsive to the guidelines, and willing to produce multiple iterations.

One of the challenges of grant writing is that the text produced must do the work of presenting the project, and so it must fulfill certain basic functions. A grant writing narrative must do the following:

- Present the project ideas clearly
- Take the reviewer through the project in an organized manner
- Include enough detail to convince the reviewer that the PI understands the basics of the implementation
- Follow the rules of grammar and style
- Be compliant to the funder's guidelines or RFP

If you have written an MA thesis or a dissertation, you can probably write a grant proposal. If you have problems with writing long papers, consider taking a writing class, even one in fiction. The important thing is that you learn to get words down on paper in a systematic way.

One of the truly helpful things about grant writing from the perspective of someone who does not like to write is that there are lots of instructions. You will not have to guess what to write because the funder will normally tell you exactly what to do.

BASIC SECTIONS OF LOIS AND GRANT PROPOSALS

Although there are many types of funders and a variety of ways to phrase a proposal, one constant in grant writing is the sections of the proposal and the general order in which they appear. Funders dictate which sections should be submitted, what they should be called, and in what order they should appear. However, most letters of interest (LOIs) and proposals have similar sections that function in similar ways. Below is a table of the standard sections of a foundation proposal or LOI. Research proposals are not much different, as we will see later in the chapter.

Section	Function for the Reader
Introduction	What I am reading?
Case/Need/Literature Review	What is the need for this project?
Project Description	What will the project accomplish?
Organization Description (Including Leadership Qualifications)	What is the nature of the organization that will be taking on this work and who is leading the project?
Conclusion	What will this project accomplish?
Project Budget	What will it cost and why?

Even when the proposal or LOI is submitted online through an application rather than as a document, these sections will appear in various forms. This chapter will cover the basics of traditional grant proposal writing, and Chapter 8 will cover online applications, including formatting issues.

LETTERS OF INTENT OR LETTERS OF INTEREST

The LOI started out as indicated by the words of the acronym: letter of intent or letter of interest. Before the Internet (and to this day with some foundations), the LOI was a letter sent by post to a funder. This letter would include an introduction of the potential grantee and a short explanation of the project. Some foundations might award based on such a letter; however, for the most part, the LOI served to convey a brief overview of the project, without requiring the more concentrated effort of a full proposal. Most often if the funder was interested in knowing more after reading the LOI, a proposal would be invited.

LOIs have changed a great deal over the last few decades. The term now refers to any sort of written request for pre-proposal consideration, including email inquiries and online pre-applications. For example, with some federal funders the LOI or NOI (notice of intent) has few technical requirements and allows the funding agency to do an effective head count to plan for the appropriate number of reviewers. When a funder requests an LOI, their guidelines should make clear the purpose of this particular document and exactly what should be submitted.

Traditional LOIs for Foundations

You probably already know several local, community-serving foundations without realizing it. Local foundations lend their names to landmarks in their communities, fund major initiatives to assist underserved populations, and bring community organizations together to tackle local problems. Most private universities and many public universities have buildings named after local foundations or their founders.

Local nonprofit organizations rely on funding from such foundations to do their work, and many faculty and university programs receive this sort of funding as well. The primary difference between research grant funding and most foundation funding is that foundations do not usually fund research per se. They fund services for the community. When a faculty or university project has a service dimension, therefore, foundation funding should be considered, and in many cases, an LOI would be prepared.

As noted above, an LOI directed toward a community-serving foundation is often a mini-proposal (generally 1–3 pages) offering an overview of the project and of the organization applying. In some cases, the funder may give the simple instruction, "Send an LOI." Other foundations may offer very specific guidelines regarding LOIs, and of course, the proposing PI should follow directions and provide what the funder asks for.

LOIs usually require the sections listed in the table on page 137. In addition, LOIs may also require a description of the following:

- Current programming
- Pending and secured funding
- Operating budget
- Board chair or president signature

Unless it is part of an online application, the LOI should be an actual, physical letter (not an email) printed on institution stationery and signed by the PI, by the dean, the president, or another similar administrator. This assures the foundation that the organization as a whole supports the project.

The LOI should be formatted as a business letter, and the sections as given in the table should not be labeled; rather they should flow together as in a traditional letter, with appropriate transitions. Budgets can be appended to this letter but are not normally included within it. It is also common to enclose institutional literature with an LOI to give the funder a broader sense of the applicant organization.

The funder may request that the LOI be executed traditionally and then scanned and attached to an email. In this case, be sure the email is written formally and use a color scanner.

Foundation Reviewers: Your Audience

Perhaps the most important item to remember when submitting an LOI (or a proposal) to a foundation for a community service project is that the "reviewers" are most likely the board of directors or a group of program officers rather than academics. They are a completely different audience from the university audience, of course, and so the documents need to be developed with these reviewers in mind.

Who Sits on the Board of Directors?

Sitting on the board of directors for a foundation (or other nonprofit) is considered an important aspect of community service and is a desirable position. It reflects leadership skills and a responsible financial commitment to the organization. The average board will contain a few of each of the following types of people:

- Members of the family of the foundation founder or the founder him- or herself, valued for carrying forward the original intent of the foundation

- Heads of companies and corporations, valued for their business acumen
- Lawyers and financial experts, valued for their skills and training
- Prominent members of the local community, often donors

This list does not normally include academics, except on research foundation boards. The board of directors carries fiduciary responsibility for a foundation, meaning that they must attend to the financial health of the organization, and they are often interested in efficiency. Naturally, finding out who sits on the board of any particular foundation is an important part of the research process before submitting an LOI or a proposal.

Sometimes proposals are reviewed by program officers and other foundation staff, who then recommend funding plans to the board. In this case, the officers may still hold a rather practical view of accomplishing community goals and may seek to make recommendations that the board will agree with.

In addition to the normal interests of reviewers in a proposal, like the soundness of the idea and clarity of the narrative, foundation board members and staff may pay attention to additional aspects of the proposal or the PI:

- **Points of contact with local organizations.** Are you working with other local organizations? Foundations often like to see collaborative projects driven by organizations with specific strengths working together. Further, colleges and universities generally have excellent financial systems, and serving as the responsible party for organizational group efforts or making financial acumen and other expertise available to these organizations may be appreciated.
- **Program evaluation.** While foundation personnel may be uninterested and sometimes even impatient with research projects, they often appreciate the evaluative aspect of social science research. It is therefore possible to perform research as part of an evaluation, and PIs who are willing to share their research acumen as evaluation may be very welcome.
- **Your networks.** Networking is an important part of the philanthropic world. Foundation staff may favor projects from PIs that are active in the community and committed to the causes they value. Take the time to get to know local foundations, go to their galas, and support their causes— and not just when you are asking for their money. In short, if you are interested in doing community work, join the community.

How to Write the LOI

If the average research proposal is written like a scholarly article, the LOI should be written like a very good piece of nonfiction. While based on facts, formal citations are not necessary. The tone can be slightly more emotional and familiar than a full proposal, especially if this is appropriate within a preexisting relationship with the funder.

Traditional LOIs are directed to busy business people or foundation personnel who read many similar letters every day. Unlike a government agency, a private funder is not required to answer every LOI or even to finish reading any particular letter. This means that writing style is a very important factor when addressing foundations.

The Introduction

Since the first sentence of an LOI may be the only sentence read, a **hook** is recommended. A hook is a writing device designed to get the reader's attention quickly and impel him to continue reading. It puts the most important aspect of the case up front and center, and it often has an emotional appeal. If you have ever received a fundraising letter or email, you have seen this kind of opening before.

For example, if I were trying to transition a successful, federally funded high school STEM education program to foundation funding, I could probably think of several different types of compelling hook sentences:

Few American children are prepared or interested in STEM careers, even though science, technology, engineering, and mathematics (STEM) jobs are projected to rise by 14 to 62 percent over the next 10 years, according to the U.S. Department of Education.

Science is perhaps the most promising area for teens to build their future careers, yet few of them are doing so.

Young people from impacted, underfunded schools rarely have the opportunity to develop their interest or ability in scientific and mathematical areas, which robs them of real economic opportunity and our community of talent.

The key is to represent your service project in one cogent sentence that appeals to the funding interests of the foundation. This sentence should be a marriage of the most essential effort of your project and the most basic concern of the foundation. What is their focus for making the world a better place? Are they interested in providing opportunities for families of low socioeconomic status? Are they interested in assisting public education? Are they interested in providing at-risk youth new choices?

The next few sentences of the LOI opening should orient the reader to the nature of the project.

> Young people from impacted, underfunded schools rarely have the opportunity to develop their interest or ability in scientific and mathematical areas, which robs them of real economic opportunity and our community of talent. The STEM Today! program, operated out of the University of the West States, is designed to help change this for hundreds of students throughout the city by providing academic assistance, personal contact with scientists and science facilities, and help with fees to take the required college entrance examinations. We are writing to ask the Foundation to consider a grant of $25,000 to STEM Today! to assist participating students with examination fees over the next two years as they apply to the colleges of their choice.

This is the introduction, short and sweet. Some people might put the "ask" (the request for funds) deeper in or save it for the end; this is a matter of preference and, perhaps, personal experience. Do keep in mind that foundations receive letters asking for money every day. They will not be shocked or surprised to see the ask placed right up front.

The Case

Next, the case must be made. Build the case like an inverted pyramid, working from the general down to the specific. Begin with what research says about community needs and work your way to the real needs facing your stakeholders. Start with commonly known aspects of the project, featuring facts and figures as reinforcement. Getting more specific to your project, use figures from the ongoing program or observations of former participants or even participants' own words to bring the point home. You can include specifics about your request in the needs section, although I tend to insert this in the project description section, as part of the solution. While some writers emphasize needs, others emphasize solutions.

> As D. N. Lee notes in her *Scientific American* blog (2013), underrepresented students from poor areas are redirected from pursuing their interests in science because of a lack of resources, discouragement from well-meaning adults, and even prevention from gate keepers. The National Center for Science and Engineering Statistics largely agrees with this list (2014), noting the importance of resources, the need for role models, and the impact of school practices, such as tracking and access to science curriculum. Even well-meaning science educators may have little success when dealing with

underrepresented populations because of cultural, resource, and experience factors.

These facts are as true in our city as anywhere else. The North West School District, home to 500,000 students, 75 percent of whom qualify for free or reduced-price lunch, features far fewer science courses per high school (4) than local, wealthier school districts (8–10). In 2011 only 3 percent of North West students passed the calculus AP exam with a score of 3 or above, and only 5 percent indicated an interest in science as a career. North West is a racially diverse district, as students are Latino (60%), African American (25%), White (10%), and Other (5%), making it an ideal locale to work toward integrating STEM fields while assisting talented, underrepresented students to move into promising careers.

Poverty impacts under-resourced children when they attempt to study science and mathematics in many ways, including the lack of resources and the lack of access to STEM role models.

Lack of Resources. STEM students from underrepresented groups often come from under-resourced families and schools. Poverty impacts science education directly, including a lack of access to scientific equipment, a lower number of science courses available at school, a lack of access to the tutoring routinely provided to more affluent students, and a lack of books, test fees, etc.

Access to STEM Role Models. Many STEM students from North West Schools lack personal contact with adults interested in and employed in STEM professions aside from their high school teachers. Personal contact with STEM workers and educators is very important for STEM students to build networks, receive mentoring, and develop self-confidence.

How should I cite D. N. Lee and the National Science Foundation (NSF)? Since reference lists are not part of business letters, use footnotes when the citation absolutely has to be made. Otherwise, simply include enough information for the material to be found in the sentence and keep your sources handy in case the funder asks for a fuller citation.

Of course, D. N. Lee's blog is not an academic source; however, as a Black woman biologist, she brings firsthand understanding of this problem, which I have backed up with an NSF document. My goal is for a board member to actually read the D. N. Lee piece, which is very accessible and may lead to a positive view of the project. Of course, a more conservative approach would be to keep the discussion of needs strictly to the NSF materials; however, this would rob the text of a human touch.

Project Description

After the case has been made, it is time to describe the project, which should sound like a perfect solution to the needs as presented.

STEM Today! was designed by Michelle Alvarez, PhD, to fill many of the gaps diverse young STEM students typically face, as indicated by educational research.

Lack of Resources. In order to help level the resource playing field, STEM Today! provides weekly tutoring in math and science subjects, as needed, helps fund scientific equipment for high school science courses, helps provide access to books and test fees, and seeks to support high school science teachers by providing undergraduate teaching assistants and access to university science faculty. Specifically, the grant we seek today will help fund student efforts to take the many examinations required to apply to STEM programs, including the SAT, SAT II, AP, and ACT tests. These funds will be applied toward exam fees as well as exam preparation. Please see the budget attachment for details on our program.

Access to STEM Role Models. The STEM Today! Program is designed to help fill the need for North West students to have personal contact with adults in STEM professions. From multiple field trips to the University of the West States, to events with university faculty, to the presence of STEM undergraduates in the high school science classroom, the program works to bring the students of North West into relationships with other STEM students and workers. STEM Today! was designed around best practices in STEM educational delivery, particularly the work of . . .

And on the letter would go.

Organization Description

The next section acquaints the foundation with the program leadership and the institution. This is not a matter of writing a simple description or inserting a pre-prepared bio. Write this section by considering the details you think the foundation personnel will be interested in. It is more important, for example, to let them know that the PI has authored several articles in top journals about STEM education than to list all publications out, because foundation staff will probably be interested in the PI's research career only as it relates to the project. They may be even more interested in leadership roles he has played, awards he has won, and other successful projects he has led.

Your institution may have a boilerplate organization description designed to be inserted into your LOI—however, be sure it conveys the most relevant information possible for the particular context you are addressing. For example, the strength of your university's STEM programs is important, but so is the outreach of STEM faculty in the community. Nobel Prize winners are wonderful, but the foundation may have real questions about the university track record of attracting and graduating underrepresented students. The huge federal grant your PI received to begin STEM Today! shows institutional success; however, the next question the funder will ask is: If you got that big federal grant, why are you asking us for money? Adapt the organizational boilerplate as necessary.

You will probably be able to get the approved institutional description from the sponsored projects officer. It may be necessary to work with her on modifying the description.

The Conclusion

The conclusion should not necessarily sum up the letter; rather, it should put a bow on it. Echo the hook, the case, or the solution rather than summarize them. Then, reiterate the ask, and invite the foundation to contact you for more information.

Treasuring the aspirations of our students, we turn to the Foundation, asking for $25,000 to help make their dreams come true. These funds will be directed toward the kind of expenses more affluent students take for granted: exam preparation, AP fees, and ordering enough score reports to go to all the colleges they apply to. These are the sort of expenses that underrepresented students often cannot afford out-of-pocket and may not even know about. In helping pave the way for diversity in science, STEM Today! helps to provide the resources, contacts, and knowledge for these students to excel and join their science peers in major university programs, giving them excellent career opportunities and helping to provide the STEM workers our country needs to face the challenges of the future. Please join us in supporting these hardworking young people.

I look forward to hearing from you.

Sincerely,

Etc.

A successful LOI will usually lead to a request for a full proposal, which is a longer, better version of the LOI, as we will explore below. Generally the letter or email requesting the proposal will provide guidelines; however, these may also be found on the foundation's website. Perhaps most importantly, the invitation to propose will include a deadline, normally within one or two months of the date of the request letter.

Much of the advice in the next section applies to foundation proposals as well as research proposals, and I will elaborate on areas that differ significantly.

STANDARD PROPOSAL STRUCTURE

Proposals are submitted to a funder under three conditions:

1. When the funder requests them through a formal announcement, usually called a request for proposals (RFP)

2. When the funder specifically requests a proposal from the PI, often (although not always) on the basis of an LOI

3. On the basis of an ongoing call for proposals featured by the funder, as with the National Institutes of Health (NIH)

As mentioned previously, among funders and across disciplines, proposals have certain basic similarities. Funders may use different labels for the sections of a proposal, but the information required is generally the same. This is because people giving money away for specific projects tend to want to know the same sorts of things:

- What will you do with the money?
- How can I trust that you will follow through properly?
- How do I know you are qualified?

The proposal structure is designed to answer these questions. The proposal sections for a research funder might look like the table below.[1]

1. Abstract/Executive Summary	What is this project basically about?
2. Literature Review/ Background/The Case	Why is it important?
3. Project Description	What will actually happen?
4. Methodology	How will knowledge be produced from it?
5. Evaluation	How will it be assessed?
6. Budget	How can we help?
7. Conclusion	Why should we fund this project?

---

[1]Proposals to traditional or nonresearch foundations may include only the case, project description, and a budget at minimum; they often have a structure very much like that of the LOI.

In addition, research funders may request the PI's biographical summary or CV.

When tackling the writing of a proposal, successful grant writers take a variety of approaches. Some start with the case, since the case defines foundation proposals. For research proposals, on the other hand, the research questions define all aspects of the project, so these should be very clear from the beginning. I personally advocate working on the logic model right after the research question and developing the budget early—because much of the project will be defined by what can and cannot be paid for and because late-budget revisions can cause havoc with submissions. Some PIs do not have a favored starting point: They simply start with the section that is most compelling to them at the moment.

Personality, work habits, and experience influence how each writer creates and sculpts the submission. The important thing is to keep your eye on the ball: Meet deadlines, accomplish tasks promptly, communicate with your team, and write, write, write!

Abstract/Executive Summary

Reviewers must read the entire length of the grant proposals they are assigned (usually 10–15 pages), and this process is easier for them when the proposal opens with a well-written abstract or executive summary. Part of the importance of the abstract/executive summary is related to the reviewing process itself. After the reviewers have read over the submissions, they often meet to discuss them and create a recommendation for funding. The ability of your reviewer to discuss and defend your proposal in this meeting will be materially helped by having a clear, interesting, and comprehensive abstract/executive summary to refer to.

The abstract or executive summary answers the question, what is this project basically about? It does not, however, simply summarize the main points of the proposal. The abstract/executive summary begins to build the argument for funding in a dynamic way that makes the reviewer actually want to read the proposal. In other words, this important first section begins the persuasion process.

The best way to persuade the reader up front is to present the most compelling and unique aspect of the proposal in the abstract/executive summary. This kind of "show-stopping" information, in fact, a type of hook, depends on the type of project and/or the discipline of the proposal, but some possible examples include the following:

- The project will help provide a unique solution to an important but under-investigated social problem.

- The project will solve a methodological problem that researchers have been struggling with for years.
- The project has the mayor's personal support, and if the pilot is successful, it will be implemented across the city.

Many proposal writers inadvertently bury this show-stopping information—the most compelling point of their projects—somewhere deep within the project descriptions. In journalism they call that "burying the lead." As you are writing and editing your project description, watch for these unique and interesting points to emerge. When you find one, be sure it is highlighted and move it up to the abstract/executive summary.

Although the abstract should include basic information about the project (see Box 7.1 on project microsummaries), do not be satisfied with copying and pasting a summary paragraph from within the proposal. Repetition is not persuasive. Write something fresh and new in the abstract. The best time to do this is probably toward the end of the writing process, after the details have been worked out and you have defined the most compelling aspects of the project.

In addition, for research proposals, be sure to include any information that gives the reviewer a strong grasp of the project: Is it quantitative or qualitative? Will it analyze an extant dataset or gather new data? Is it lab based or field based? What is the basic methodology? What are the research questions? What is the expected result of the project? What are the broader impacts of the project, or how will this project make the world a better place?

When an abstract is not required, it is strongly recommended that the PI still use a paragraph or two at the beginning of the narrative to provide a short executive summary as a way of opening the proposal. This paragraph should accomplish the same important work the abstract would do, perhaps in a more concise way.

Box 7.1   Your Project Objectives Are Not Obvious

I have read many proposals featuring excellent objectives that are not stated until several pages into the narrative, and sometimes they are not stated at all. The words that go through my mind are, "Yes, but what do you want to do?" Perhaps the research questions are not stated up front, or the outcome is not defined in the first page. Perhaps the literature review goes on and on, quoting everyone in the discipline, and I am left thinking, "Yes, but what do you want to do?"

One way to make the project objectives up front and clear to the reader is to create a microsummary of the project. A **microsummary** is a two-sentence description that captures the nature of project activities. Work this into two or three places throughout the proposal: the executive summary or abstract, the introductory paragraph of the project description, perhaps the conclusion or even the budget justification.

Which of the following microsummary samples is more explicit? Which one are you more likely to remember?

- The project will provide an understanding of how former inmates re-adapt to society by interviewing them. In order to conduct this study, the PI has created the POWER Collaborative, which will provide screening and access to potential participants who may wish to join the program.
- This longitudinal project is designed to provide an understanding of how former inmates re-adapt to society through ongoing interviews, focus groups, and monitoring of their relationships with parole officers. In order to conduct this study, the PI has created the POWER Collaborative, made up of five community organizations that seek to serve and support this population and help assist former inmates create new lives in society.

Why is Sample 2 more effective? What did I do differently? I added more information to help the reader quickly understand this project. Specifically, the reader now knows that the project is:

Longitudinal—We will get to know this population over time.

Qualitative—There will be personal interaction and a great deal of detail.

Community based—Five organizations support the POWER Collaborative.

Literature Review/Background/The Case

Traditional foundation grant writers often call it "the case" or "background," and research funders may call it the "literature review." Whatever you call it, this section explains why the project is necessary.

The differences in naming reflect the interests of foundations and research organizations and the distinct ways they take in information. The educated laymen who run most foundations are dedicated to solving social problems and are often already familiar with the case or the situation presented. They want to know the details and what the applicant thinks will solve the problem. They will accept information from a fairly wide variety of sources, as long as these are familiar and socially acceptable (i.e., *The New York Times* rather than a club newsletter and scholarly research presented in the appropriate language).

On the other hand, federal agencies, research foundations, and scholarly affinity organizations reflect scholarly practice. Program officers, boards, and the faculty who serve on review committees seek to know more about the need for the project by a presentation of the relevant peer-reviewed literature. Research organizations therefore tend to accept a more narrow range of sources, and information from these sources needs to be formally cited as in a journal submission. The need for the research project is not just social need; it may be scientific need, as in an area that needs exploration, or a methodological need, as in a new technique that needs to be tested.

Background/The Case

We have discussed the case previously in the LOI section; however, the LOI touches on the need for the project in a few paragraphs. The proposal provides rich detail as it builds the platform for presentation of the project.

Following are some suggestions for writing an excellent case.

Remember that the case is an essential part of the persuasion process. Include facts and details that you think will persuade the reader to fund your project. You do not have to include every detail: Choose details that are related to your project and your solution.

Use an inverted pyramid structure to present material. Initial points should reflect general understandings of the problem. As the description goes on, the facts should become more and more specific, and local.

Provide "citations" within sentences. For example, "*The New York Times* recently reported (May 26, 2013) that the increase of homelessness brought on by the Great Recession appears to be a permanent situation."[2] Only cite when you absolutely have to.

Carefully insert details in the description to make the situation come alive for the reader. For example, "Night after night, hundreds of homeless families,

---

[2]As with most of the examples I give in this book, this "citation" is fabricated.

shuddering from the cold, join the staff of the Family Care Shelter for a place to sleep and a warm meal."

"Alex, a second-year participant in the STEM Today! program, looks down as he quietly describes the difficulties he faces in trying to find a quiet place to study in the home he shares with five siblings."

Gather local statistics on the program. How many people have you served? What sort of difficulties did they face before they joined your program? What other resources are available (or not available) to them?

Present the case in such a way that your proposed project ameliorates the need as you have described it. The best case descriptions are like narrative questions that the project description later answers. They are problems that the project description solves.

The Literature Review

The literature review is somewhat different. There are many fine books on writing literature reviews, and the reader who does not have a firm sense of how to present a literature review in his discipline is urged to consult one of these, his advisor, or the relevant professional group (i.e., the ASA, AERA, APA, etc.). What is presented here are literature review basics for grants prepared for those who can already write a literature review.

Grant literature reviews are generally far shorter than those for journals, so they must be direct and to the point. The grant literature review is not designed to demonstrate the PI's command of the scholarly literature; that should be obvious from the PI's publications, which will be provided via the CV or biosketch. The grant literature review exists to provide a venue for the PI to explain why the project should be funded. Keeping in mind that in scholarly fields information only counts once it has been peer reviewed, only peer-reviewed literature on the topic can support the PI's claims that the project is relevant and important. The existing body of scholarly literature offers directions about what is known, unknown, and not fully known, and in this way, it points toward what areas need more work and are thus potential grant projects. Consider, for example, whether a study would be funded if there were already ten of the same peer-reviewed studies in existence. Obviously, the eleventh study would be rejected unless it had a completely different angle on the problem.

The literature review, therefore, is an extension of the persuasion process. It will indicate the most important aspects of what is known already and what is not known about the topic. As with the case, be sure that the literature review is relevant to the project description. If possible, limit your discussion of what is not known about the topic to those parts your project will address.

Performing a literature review in one or two pages is a challenge; therefore, it is important to address some important stressors.

What should I include?

Include the minimal discussion of the most necessary sources to prove your points sufficiently. Be aware of disciplinary subtexts in this situation and use them to your advantage. For example, if by citing a specific author you are really calling up an entire school of thought, then just cite that author. Save the space and let the reviewers fill the rest in mentally.

Where do I come down in disciplinary controversies?

Because you cannot control who will review your submission, an even-handed, middle-of-the-road take on controversies is recommended. It is entirely possible to have a reviewer whose point of view is very different from your own, so be judicious.

Who should I cite?

This is a question of primary importance. As with journals, it is possible to offend reviewers who feel their work should have been cited in your study, so it is probably better to pay more attention to living scholars who can become annoyed than to dead giants in the field. Be cautious and do a little research. It may be possible to find out whether certain scholars are closely associated with various programs and agencies, making contact with them more probable. Sometimes you can ask that certain scholars be included or excluded from your review panel, but these requests will not always be honored.

Project Description

The project description is the heart of the proposal. This section should clearly explicate how the project will work, who will run it, and if there is no separate "outcome" section required in the proposal, what will happen as a result of the grant. A well-structured proposal will set up the need for the project in the literature review/background/the case and offer a solution for those needs in the project description.

While a variety of formats can be followed in the project description, one variant might conceptually look something like Figure 7.1. The easiest way to write the project description is to base it on the logic model as previously discussed in Chapter 5 and Case Study 1.

In the first paragraph, the scope of the project should be briefly explored, and the research questions or goals should be stated simply and directly, especially if

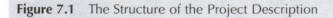

Figure 7.1   The Structure of the Project Description

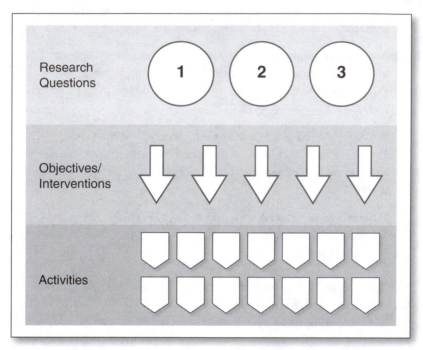

Does this look familiar? This structure lines up with the simple logic model discussed in Chapter 5.

they have not appeared already. These will be related to the upcoming objectives or interventions and can be related to the already-stated needs or the context as established in the literature review or case. The first paragraph of the project description is a good place to include your microsummary (Box 7.1) if you have one.

Note that you have already described the need for the project in the previous section. This leaves you free to dig into the details of the project description. In this section, you should present your vision of how the project will operate. It is not enough to state what the project will accomplish; you must offer a description of *how* the project will accomplish the tasks you set out.

Below are some areas to consider as you create a project description. This is not a list of sections to include; rather, these are questions you must answer for yourself in order to write about the administrative nature of your project successfully.

What is the leadership structure of the project?

Is there an advisory committee? Is the PI completely in charge? Who is responsible for day-to-day operations? Larger projects should create a short management plan for the reviewers to consider.

Are you hiring employees?

Be sure to include them and their roles in the project description. Consider that you are in fact justifying lines in the budget as you explain their roles.

What people and offices will project personnel interact with?

How will you contact them? Is there a recruitment process? Do you need to enter into agreements with other offices in order to implement the project?

What would an actual day on your project look like?

Where will the work take place? Who will participate? How do your tasks translate to real world activity?

These questions may seem obvious to you as the writer or PI, but they will not be obvious to the reviewers.

The best way to get everything on paper is just to get everything on paper! Follow your logic model, create an outline, and start with a complete description of everything that will happen. Once you have written all of this out, you can decide what needs to stay and what can be cut. Many PIs are surprised to realize, at the end of this process, that there are aspects of the project they themselves have not fully worked out yet.

Common problems often associated with project description sections include the following:

- **The project description is too vague.** In this case, the reader cannot get a sense of what will actually happen if the project is awarded.
- **The description has not been worked out carefully.** As a result, there are logical inconsistencies and evidence of poor planning.
- **The description is not aligned with the budget.** There are things discussed in the project description that are not budgeted out, and things in the budget that do not seem to play a part in the project.

Below is a model project description based on the project we discussed in Chapter 6, which will give you a sense of section organization and the kind of detail that is helpful to the reviewer.

Project Description

The Teaching STEM Subjects in Introductory University Courses (Teaching STEM)[3] project has been designed to study the effect of alternative learning techniques on the university STEM classroom we ask two research questions:

    1. Does the use of alternative learning techniques improve student retention of content in science courses?

    2. Does the use of alternative learning techniques affect the time required for faculty to prepare for their courses?

These questions will be investigated by the PI, Robert Miller, with the assistance of the Co-PI, Mahmud Jamal, and 15 faculty participants at the Californian Comprehensive University who have agreed to incorporate alternative learning techniques into one introductory STEM course each per year. Additionally, local PIs from Large Public University (Linda Johnson) and Small Liberal Arts College (Alex Gonzalez) will carry out the same investigation on their own campuses with seven and eight faculty participants each, respectively. This project will include a two-year cycle of curriculum development and deployment, annual participant workshops to review findings and encourage conversation on project progress, and an extensive evaluation process to ensure that the creative alignment structure remains intact.

    1. Does the use of alternative learning techniques improve student retention of content in science courses?

Participating faculty members will be provided with resources to develop a curriculum for one introductory science course that includes consistent, systematic use of Alternative Learning techniques. Techniques adopted must create dialog with and/or among students during classroom presentations and must account for an average of 50 percent of class time (with the other 50 percent as lecture, if the instructor wishes).

Faculty collaborators will have the choice of which alternative learning techniques are adopted, under the guidance of three experts

---

[3]Many PIs go to some trouble to create interesting acronyms. When this works it is very good, but when it does not it can lead to strained titles. Instead of an acronym, one can use a shortened title as in this example.

(Continued)

(Continued)

(Hsieh Da-Xia, Tom Murray, and Françoise Albert). Participating faculty will choose from relatively established techniques that are considered best practices for their disciplines and will be adapted to the university setting in consultation with one of the project experts. Techniques can include in-class discussions between students, use of clickers, student investigative or problem-solving teams, students teaching each other concepts, and so forth. Faculty will be encouraged to prepare for and give the same final exam as the one offered in their traditional lecture and lab courses.

One interesting aspect of this study is that it will be employed in relatively small courses (less than 30 students) at Small Liberal Arts College, large lecture courses at Large Public University (average introductory science class size approximately 90 students), and a mixture of these at Californian Comprehensive University (22–100 students each). In order to facilitate comparison, courses will be categorized as follows:

Small	10–29 students
Medium	30–49 students
Large	50+ students

The structure of the intervention includes a two-year cycle.

Year 1: Control Year. Each faculty member will teach the first year in the traditional lecture/lab format while measuring student achievement with project instruments at the prescribed times. Faculty will evaluate student learning through pre- and posttesting at specified intervals (four times per year) using assessments developed specifically for each course under the supervision of learning consultants. Toward the end of each semester, students will be given a questionnaire developed by project personnel to ascertain their opinions on the nature of the pedagogy in use that semester. Faculty will also be interviewed twice per year by program staff on the progress of the course: once in the first three weeks, and once after the course is over.

Over the first summer, faculty will meet at organized workshops to share their observations, engage in professional development, and plan the next year's alternative learning styles curriculum. At this time, each faculty member will formally choose his or her alternative learning techniques for use in the upcoming year and begin adapting these to the course. There will be bi-weekly follow-up meetings throughout the rest of the summer to assist faculty members with completing the curriculum plans, and each plan will be approved by the PI as appropriate for inclusion in the study.

Year 2: Initial Alternative Learning Year. Each faculty member will teach the same course over the next year using alternative learning techniques included in the curriculum plan developed over the previous summer with the assistance of program staff and educational consultants. Faculty will be at liberty to choose which techniques to apply, and to plan them out—although once the curriculum is set, major divergences from it will need to be approved by the PI in order to ensure consistency.

During the pedagogical phase, student achievement will be monitored with the same project instruments as in Year 1, at similarly prescribed times. Pre- and posttesting four times per year, as well as twice yearly faculty interviews will be held. Faculty will have access to educational program staff for support using the collaborative techniques while teaching, as well as access to educational consultants, as needed. Over the summer, faculty will meet to share their experiences and to compare notes on what worked and why. Each faculty member will contribute data and other written materials toward the final report.

During both years, 15 students participating in the classrooms will be randomly selected for in-depth interviews on learning in STEM fields and pursuing STEM majors and careers. Student reflection on their classroom experience will not only provide depth to the study, but will help inform faculty as they pursue the next iterations of their lesson plans.

Question 2: Does the use of alternative learning techniques affect the time required for faculty to prepare for their courses?

This is an important question for faculty who are considering embarking on the kind of deep-seated changes to the curriculum that alternative learning represents. Across academia, faculty members are expected to spend significant time on student advising, committee work, various departmental roles, and their own research in addition to

(Continued)

(Continued)

teaching. The writing of the alternative learning curriculum represents a new course for each faculty member, and may entail a large time commitment during the first year. On the other hand, since faculty will not spend as much time lecturing, will the nature of preparation time change?

To measure this, faculty will be asked to answer a short online questionnaire (three questions) whenever they are engaged in course preparation activities, including during the summer preparation workshops for both years of the study. They will also be asked to assign a code to their preparation activity: reading, grading, creating written student material (including photocopying), planning collaborative activities, training TAs, or answering student questions about the course. There will also be a notes section in the questionnaire where faculty can log their observations throughout the semester.

During the twice yearly interviews, each faculty member will be asked about his or her impressions of the preparation process, including the time involved, how different the preparation was from other previously taught courses, and personal opinions about the alternative learning process in general.

Methodology

The methodology section is intrinsic to research proposals, because this is where the PI explains the steps she will take in her research. In small projects (which fund only the investigator) the methodology may even fulfill the function of the project description. Like project descriptions, methodology sections in research proposals must be robust and well developed. Their function is not only to explain to the reviewer what will be done but also to convey the PI's familiarity with the techniques to be used.

As such, robust methodology sections go beyond listing survey questions. They discuss recruiting processes, experimental and quasi-experimental protocols, the statistical tests that will be applied to the data, why these have been chosen, how the data will be handled, procedures for maintaining participant confidentiality, and more. For better or worse, the methodology section demonstrates to the reviewer the PI's comfort level with the research protocol and with best practices in data management. A good methodology section instills confidence that the research will be handled responsibly and scientifically, making the project a good investment in the pursuit of knowledge.

There are a wide range of research methodologies in the social sciences, and many good books describing best practices for executing them. The reader is advised to consult with the relevant disciplinary professional group to find the best titles for the project at hand. However, below are a few guidelines for writing a methodology section.

Include the formal names for the research methods you will use. If you have put together a procedure and do not have a formal name for it, invest some time with a methodology book to figure out what the formal name would be. For example, rather than admitting that you will not be pretesting your participants, you could explain that you will be using a static-group comparison and why this is the best possible quasi-experimental design for your project. Not only does this make a stronger case, but as you study experimental design, you may also find out a thing or two that will help you create a better project.

Carefully consider the use of a control group, even if this is difficult to arrange. A control group will lend credence to your results. You may not have to form a control yourself: If you know of a project working with a similar demographic to your group of interest, perhaps they would allow you to survey their participants. A control group can also be created using secondary data.

Explain and justify your sampling plan. Similar to your research design, find the formal way to describe how you will choose people to gather data from and justify your selection process as the best way to conduct your research. For example, if you are doing a qualitative study of a small group of people who are spread out in the population, you may have to ask each informant for information leading to the next informant. This is called snowball sampling, a nonprobability method that is perfectly legitimate when justified appropriately.

Describe the nature of the raw data you will gather and how you will prepare them for analysis. Who will input the data? How will you verify that the data were recorded correctly? Could missing data be a problem, and if so, what will you do to handle it?

Name the software and analytical techniques you intend to use. Demonstrate to the reviewer that you know what you are doing. If you are not really sure about the correct techniques, work with your advisor or befriend someone with more statistical acumen in order to make this section shine. The fact is, once you are done with the project, you will know what you are doing, so think toward that goal.

All of these tips are just as important for qualitative researchers, especially when proposing to a funder that emphasizes quantitative research. Explain clearly why your qualitative technique is the best way to explore the issue, be exact and detailed about the methodology, and be judicious; write to your audience in a persuasive way.

Avoid these common pitfalls when writing the methodology section:

There is not enough detail. As a result, reviewers do not have a solid understanding of the project and therefore points are deducted or they cannot recommend it for funding.

The PI thinks of the analysis as an appendage to the project, whereas the analysis is the heart of most research projects. The project may involve a great deal of activity in fieldwork, setting up experiments, and surveying people; however, none of that will mean anything unless the data are analyzed well. Develop your methodology and analysis with the same care as the rest of the project.

Too much detail is included. On the other hand, there are highly quantitatively skilled PIs who include methodology sections with such specific language that the reviewers have trouble understanding what is being proposed. Reviewers may not be from your area or even from your discipline, so keep methodology sections jargon free and seek balance in detail.

Box 7.2 is an example of an excellent methodology section composed by Michael Gottfried, PhD, of UC Santa Barbara for his project *Career and Technical Education as a Foundation to Support Postsecondary Transitions in STEM for Students with Disabilities,* which was awarded in 2012 by the National Science Foundation (NSF). Note the detail that Gottfried includes, even down to Table 1.

Box 7.2   Analytic Approach

Our analysis will first involve a descriptive overview of the CTE[4] landscape in high school. We will document which aspects of the CTE experience are most common among students with disabilities, when during high school

---
[4]Career and Technical Education

students engage in these activities, and in what combination. In addition to providing basic information on CTE, this initial analysis will provide the foundation for an empirical test of the efficacy of CTE on post-secondary STEM outcomes—the main objective of our analysis. We will apply multivariate, quasi-experimental regression techniques to discern whether STEM course-taking, school-based work programs, formal labor market experience, or any combination puts students in the best position to adopt STEM majors in college and/or take jobs that incorporate STEM skills and concepts. In all of our analyses that require tests of significance, we will adjust our standard errors using Taylor-series linearization methods to account for the clustered and stratified sampling design of the data. We will also use probability weights to adjust our estimates for sampling and item non-response. Also, we will examine the extent of missing data on critical items in our analysis, and explore imputation techniques, if necessary. We discuss our analytic strategy for each research question in turn.

Research Question 1: What CTE experiences are provided to students with disabilities during high school?

First, we will descriptively explore the distributions of students' CTE experiences in the ELS:2002 sample. Table 1 shows an example of how the data will be organized for the analysis of STEM course taking, using the ELS data.

In the rows of this table, we will list each of the courses that are classified as STEM courses. We will then tabulate the percentage of the sample who ever earned credit in any STEM course and then the percentage of the sample that earned credit in each STEM course (e.g. surveying, computer science, etc.).[5] We will conduct a similar analysis for school-based employment programs and labor force employment.

Our tabulations, exemplified by Table 1, will also include columns that will show the timing of the CTE experiences. For example, among those who earned credit in surveying, we will calculate the percentage that earned that credit in 11th grade, and so on. We will calculate this for each type of CTE: STEM course taking, school-based employment, and labor force participation.

---

[5]In the SST, there are approximately 50 courses classified as engineering technologies and 40 courses classified as computer/information sciences.

(Continued)

(Continued)

Table 1   Percentage Earning Credit in STEM Courses

	Percent Earning Credits	Earned Credit in 11th Grade	Earned Credit in 12th Grade

STEM
    Surveying
    Computer Science
    Course Title
    Course Title
    Etc.			

Of course, this methodology section goes on to discuss each research question in detail.

Evaluation

The evaluation section explains how the project will be monitored for the performance promised in the proposal. This is extremely important for all parties concerned: The PI wants to finish the project successfully and on time; the funder wants the work to be accomplished as promised; and the university is liable for use of the funds. The evaluation is like a local research project dedicated to investigating the project itself.

The evaluation section, therefore, is related to and mirrors the methodology section. The evaluation section has research questions, information on data collection and management, and analytical techniques. Small projects tend to have internal evaluations run by the PI, in which case the evaluation section demonstrates how the PI will monitor the project for compliance to grant terms and to the goals of the project. Large projects may hire an external evaluator with a team of people to monitor the project.

The key to a good evaluation is integrating the evaluation efforts into the working processes of the project. Evaluation is common to large service projects funded by federal agencies; however, for research projects the concept of evaluation may seem odd. After all, is the research project not a type of evaluation? Yet some funders will require an evaluation of a research project. In either case, when evaluation is planned, keep the following in mind:

- Bring the evaluator on early and integrate evaluation processes with the day-to-day business of the project. This means that the evaluator should attend major project meetings both before and after a grant award.
- Give the evaluator access to research data.
- Collect data from the very beginning of the project.
- Pay attention to the data collected to find and deal with potential problems efficiently.

If you are required to set up an evaluation for a small research project, consider appropriately sized measures that might help assure the funder that you are managing things well. For example:

- Create an advisory committee of senior faculty, industry professionals, or stakeholders to meet and review project progress once or twice per year.
- Involve your advisor or other mentor with the grant for a week each summer to go over project progress in detail and report to the foundation. It is normally acceptable to pay such a person for a week or two of effort in this context.
- Hire a senior graduate student from a social science discipline who is interested in starting a career in evaluation. If you are from a predominantly undergraduate institution, you might reach out to local research universities.

The evaluation section is as big a promise as the rest of the grant proposal, so anything mentioned here that will cost money needs to find its way into the budget and needs to be integrated into project implementation. Even though the evaluation implementation is explained separately in the proposal, it is important for the project team to treat evaluation as part of general implementation—and even better, to plan it that way.

If you are writing the evaluation section, be sure to include both formative and summative analysis. The **formative analysis** is ongoing during project implementation and designed to ensure that the plan is being followed. Excellent evaluations detail how formative feedback will be presented to project leaders and how it will be acted upon when project performance needs to be improved.

Summative analysis provides the final word on project implementation and is generally submitted to the funder at the end of the funding period. For some projects, the summative analysis is simply the final report, including a financial report indicating how funds were spent and a narrative or technical report offering data to support project outcomes.

Budget

The budget will generally be requested in the guidelines, often with a budget justification. Look back to Chapter 6 for more information on preparing the budget.

Conclusion

Some grant submissions do not have conclusions. They simply end with the last section, often evaluation or methodology. Page limitations may dictate this. Yet if there is space, it is always helpful to include one or two concluding paragraphs to renew the reviewer's sense of the project. This is especially helpful in cases when the really interesting project description came ten pages earlier.

The conclusion should not be a mere summary; it should hit the high notes of the proposal once more by echoing the most salient aspects of the project. The conclusion is also a great place to echo the hook or perhaps reiterate some version of the microsummary.

Sometimes the structure dictated by the funder works very well to provide a natural conclusion. For example, the NSF requires sections addressing intellectual merit (how the project builds our knowledge of an area, process, or methodology) and broader impacts (how the project will change a discipline, population, context, the world, etc.). Ending the proposal with a soaring broader impacts section is a wonderful way to provide a memorable conclusion without repetition; and whether they are required or not, broader impacts are a welcome addition to any grant proposal.

USING A RUBRIC TO STRUCTURE THE PROPOSAL

If you find a **rubric** in the RFP, pay attention. A rubric is a written guide for how your proposal will be scored, and if you have one, you should use it to structure your proposal. Federal, state, and municipal funders often include rubrics, as do some foundations. Below is a fictionalized example based on a federal agency rubric.

1. Meets the purpose of program (up to 20 points)

   A. Promotes interdisciplinary collaboration
   B. Contributes to the development of a pool of experts to meet national needs
   C. Promotes access to resulting research

2. Need for project is great (up to 15 points)

   A. The need for the services to be provided
   B. The extent to which specific gaps or weaknesses in services, infrastructure, or opportunities have been identified and will be addressed by the proposed project

3. Significance (up to 10 points)

   A. The national significance of the proposed project
   B. The local significance of the proposed project

4. Quality of the project design (up to 10 points)

   A. The extent to which the design of the proposed project is appropriate to and will successfully address the needs of the target population or other identified needs
   B. The extent to which the proposed activities constitute a coherent, sustained program
   C. The extent to which the goals, objectives, and outcomes to be achieved by the proposed project are clearly specified and measurable
   D. The extent to which the proposed project represents an exceptional approach to the priority or priorities established for the competition

5. Quality of project services (up to 10 points)

   A. The quality and sufficiency of strategies for ensuring equal access and treatment for eligible project participants who are members of groups that have traditionally been underrepresented based on race, color, national origin, gender, age, or disability
   B. The extent to which the services to be provided by the proposed project are appropriate to the needs of the intended recipients or beneficiaries of those services

6. Quality of project personnel (up to 10 points)

   A. The extent to which the applicant encourages applications for employment from persons who are members of groups that have traditionally been underrepresented based on race, color, national origin, gender, age, or disability
   B. The qualifications, including relevant training and experience, of key project personnel

7. Adequacy of resources (up to 10 points)

   A. The extent to which the budget is adequate to support the proposed project

   B. The extent to which the costs are reasonable in relation to the number of persons to be served and to the anticipated results and benefits

8. Quality of the project evaluation (up to 15 points)

   A. The extent to which the methods of evaluation are appropriate to the context within which the project operates

   B. The extent to which the methods of evaluation include the use of objective performance measures that are clearly related to the intended outcomes of the project and will produce quantitative and qualitative data to the extent possible

There is a great deal of valuable structural information provided by this rubric. For example, it defines what sections to include and what to write about in each section. The wording of the rubric section titles should be used as proposal section headings because the reviewers will most likely be using this rubric to rate the proposal. If some rubric section titles are wordy, reduce them to more conventional but related titles that are easier to read quickly.

In addition, based on the rubric you can ascertain the relative length of each section by figuring out what percentage of the entire proposal the points represent, then converting this to pages (see Box 7.3, Rubric Conversion Table).

Box 7.3   Rubric Conversion Table

Item	Points[1]	Percentage[2]	Pages[3]
1. Meets the purpose of the program	20	20%	5
2. Need for project	15	15%	3.75
3. Significance	10	10%	2.5
4. Quality of the project design	10	10%	2.5
5. Quality of project services	10	10%	2.5
6. Quality of project personnel	10	10%	2.5

Item	Points[1]	Percentage[2]	Pages[3]
7. Adequacy of resources (The budget is not included in page limit, so consider these pages free.)	10	10%	2.5
8. Quality of the project evaluation	15	15%	3.75
Totals	100	100%	25

[1] Points were derived from the rubric presented in the RFP.

[2] Points/100

[3] Percentages × 25

Converting the assigned points into pages helps the PI to address each section efficiently, in accordance with the funder's priorities. Note that Section 1, Meets the Purpose of the Program, is the largest prescribed section at five pages. Significant time must be spent, therefore, in relating the project to the purpose of the grant program as defined by the funder. The next two largest sections are Section 2, Need for Project, and Section 8, Quality of Project Evaluation, at 3.75 pages each. The length of the project evaluation section, in particular, should cause the PI to pause and reflect. It is obvious that the funder will consider evaluation an important part of the proposal, so the PI should be ready to produce a robust evaluation section.

WORKING WITH YOUR SPONSORED PROJECTS OFFICE

At some institutions, sponsored projects officers may assist faculty and university personnel with foundation proposals and LOIs, and at other colleges and universities these may be handled by corporate and foundation relations officers. When applying to a foundation, check in with sponsored projects to determine the appropriate office to work with.

If you are working with the sponsored projects office and the foundation requires that the LOI be signed by the board chair or president, it is very important to discuss this early. You will need to know the protocol for submitting such a letter to the president's office, and it is very likely that you will need to submit it early for review. In the absence of a sponsored projects office, corporate and foundation relations or development should be contacted to provide such a signature.

WORKING WITH THE CORPORATE AND FOUNDATION RELATIONS OFFICE

Proposals and LOIs to foundations are primarily the work of corporate and foundation relations. This is what development grant writing staff and officers work on day in and day out, and they are probably very well acquainted with local foundation personnel. Lean on this knowledge, especially in terms of relationship building. The average corporate and foundation relations officer will have a lot to teach you about foundation fundraising.

Beware, however, of any offer to write the proposal or LOI for you. While development grant writers are masters of this sort of expression, they may not fully understand your research, and they may be willing to make compromises that could endanger your outcomes. Work with them closely and remember that corporate and foundation relations and development officers are some of the most singularly dedicated people you will find at a college or university. They want you to succeed and they will do their best, in their own way, to help you accomplish your fundraising goals.

THE NUTS & BOLTS

1. An LOI is a way of communicating initial interest in submitting a proposal to the funder. It may take the form of a letter, email, or online application.

2. The basic proposal structure includes the following sections: executive summary/abstract, literature review/background/the case, project description, methodology, evaluation, and budget.

3. When writing each section of the proposal, focus on the purpose of the section. Do not try to fit the literature review in the project description, for example.

4. If the funder offers information on how the proposal will be evaluated or a rubric, use this to structure the proposal. Label sections clearly.

5. Follow directions!!

EXERCISES: WORKING TOWARD MASTERY

1. Using the logic model you created for Chapter 5, create an outline of the project description for your narrative. Feel free to review Case Study 1 to see how a logic model can be converted to an outline.

2. Create outline content for the following additional proposal sections:

- Executive Summary/Abstract
- Literature Review/Background/The Case
- Methodology
- Evaluation
- Conclusion

If you have a funder in mind, use the guidelines provided.

CHAPTER TERMS

Formative analysis: Evaluation process that helps the PI to keep the grant running according to plan.

Hook: A sentence or two at the beginning of a letter or proposal designed to catch the reader's interest.

Microsummary: About two sentences that express what the project will really do. Memorable microsummaries give the reader a visceral sense of the project.

Rubric: A written guide with a list of criteria to score a grant proposal.

Summative analysis: Evaluation process demonstrating that a project has accomplished all of its goals. Summative analysis is most often directed to the funder in a final report.

8

Grants.gov and Other Online Applications

INTRODUCTION

An online proposal is usually an Internet-based application that allows the applicant to convey proposal information to the funder electronically. More and more foundation applications and almost all federal applications are now primarily or completely online. Online applications require the traditional grant writing skills we have explored, but they also require proficiency in various software packages and the ability to write and edit concisely.

Online grant application processes vary depending on the funder. As you will find out, some are very well engineered and relatively straightforward, and others are not. Some have great support and help pages, and others do not. There are three general things to keep in mind when working with online applications:

1. **Follow directions.**

    Online application processes may happen quickly, and you may not be able to double-check your work before submitting. It is extremely important to pay attention to any and all guidelines offered.

2. **Expect technical glitches.**

    By "glitch" I mean anything that happens with the online application that you do not expect. For example, some applications do not warn you when you have gone over the maximum character length for a field. They just cut off your response. Naturally, glitches also include cases of actual software and equipment malfunction.

3. **Begin the submission process three workdays before the deadline.**

   This means that you should have the application filled out and ready to submit at least three days before the deadline. You may have to complete the application several times, or you may run into a series of complications and need to call technical assistance. A three-day window allows enough time to resolve problems and submit before the deadline.

In this chapter we will cover Grants.gov, primarily because it is the main application portal for many federal agencies and because it provides examples of the kind of glitches that can occur with online applications.

WHAT IS GRANTS.GOV?

Grants.gov is both a submission portal and an online clearinghouse of federal grant information. Many (but not all) of the 26 federal agencies that list grant opportunities on Grants.gov also use the site to receive submissions. Like many government projects, Grants.gov must serve many constituents, so it is clunky—like driving a very large, old car.

Each agency that accepts submissions through Grant.gov uses the forms a little differently. This means it is important to pay attention to agency instructions about completing the forms, even if these do not seem to make sense to you.

A Grants.gov submission is different from other online applications because you do not fill out forms posted on a website. Instead, you download an application package to your computer. The application package is an electronic file of documents that must be opened and filled out with Adobe Reader. In addition, your own documents, such as the narrative, CVs, budget justification, and letters of support, must be uploaded to the application package itself. Once you complete the application, you will submit it through directions and buttons within the package. Although all of this may sound very abstract, it will become obvious once you actually open an application package and explore it a little.

Box 8.1 True Story

Fewer people complain about Grants.gov today than they did a decade ago. In fact, when I first started as a grants administrator, I belonged to a listserv that functioned primarily as an unofficial complaint line and self-help service for Grants.gov users, most of whom were other grants administrators.

Grants.gov would inexplicably become unavailable, questions would go unanswered, and applicants would receive mysterious error messages like "broken pipe"—messages familiar to database experts but completely mysterious to grants people like me. It is not an exaggeration to say that there were grants administrators at some universities who became Grants.gov specialists—just because the site was that difficult to work with at times!

Grants.gov has improved tremendously over the last few years. "Broken pipe" messages are a thing of the past, submissions have become easier and more dependable, and help line staff are very knowledgeable and provide good assistance.

GETTING HELP

When getting help with an online application submission, keep in mind that the people employed to maintain the online application are generally not the same as the people who run the grant program. This is true for foundations, which often outsource online applications, and it is certainly true of Grants.gov, which is run by the Department of Health and Human Services (DHHS) as a separate department. This means that when you run into trouble while working on an online submission, it is important to consider the nature of the problem before you seek assistance.

Contact the agency or funder (after checking the guidelines) if you have questions about the guidelines, about the content of the documents to be submitted, or about narrative or budget requirements.

Contact the technical people who run the online application if the website is not functioning properly or if you have questions about its features, how to upload documents, or other technical issues.

There is usually a section of the application website that answers common questions (Frequently Asked Questions, FAQs) or a help page. Well-developed applications have robust help pages, and you can often get your questions answered there. Many funders have technical assistance that is only available during traditional work hours (Monday through Friday, from 8:30 a.m. to 5 p.m.).

The updated Grants.gov website is very navigable and offers several pages of help files. In addition, you can call and talk to a live person 24 hours a day, 7 days a week (except federal holidays). If you run into a problem within three days before submission and cannot find an answer, it is very important to call Grants.gov immediately and get your question answered. When you call in, the technician will give you a case number, which you should copy and keep. This way, if your submission is late because of a technical problem that was out of your control, you may still have your proposal considered for that particular competition.

Box 8.2   Adobe Reader and Grants.gov

Grants.gov applications are only compatible with specific versions of Adobe Reader. While Adobe Professional is a great tool, it is very important that PIs only open the Grants.gov application with Adobe Reader—in fact, the same version of Adobe Reader that the entire grants team is using. If you open the package with any other program, even for a second, you will not be able to submit it. This includes opening the file by mistake and closing it quickly without typing anything. That small mistake will cause the file to become unsubmittable.

So even if it seems unnecessary, follow all directions on the Grants. gov website about using Adobe Reader, including changing your computer's PDF preferences to Adobe Reader.

HOW DO I GET STARTED WITH GRANTS.GOV?

Most people get started with Grants.gov by searching for grants on the Grants.gov website. Some funding agencies have search facilities and guidelines available on their own websites; others offer the bulk of their information on Grants.gov through specific competitions. Some agencies, like the Department of Education, use Grants. gov for some of their submissions and not for others. Sometimes, as with the National Science Foundation (NSF), opportunities are posted to Grants.gov and applicants are asked to submit elsewhere (FastLane). Pay attention to the request for proposals (RFP) and any other documents you may find to determine how best to submit your proposal. If you have never submitted to a particular agency before, cross-check information on both Grants.gov and the agency website.

Once you identify an opportunity of interest (we covered opportunity selection in Chapter 3 and Chapter 4), click on the Opportunity link on the Grants.gov site to see the guidelines. On the Synopsis Detail page, be sure to sign up for change notification emails to keep up with any alterations to the competition. You can download the application on the Application Package page. Remember to follow the directions regarding the use of Adobe Reader.

Different agencies use the Grants.gov application differently—there is no uniform set of directions across agencies. Some agencies will offer limited information about their requirements on Grants.gov and will simply tell you to fill out the application. Others, like the National Institutes of Health (NIH), have developed extremely specific directions for working with submissions through Grants. gov. Look diligently for directions and guidelines and follow these carefully.

MISCELLANEOUS ISSUES
ASSOCIATED WITH GRANTS.GOV SUBMISSIONS

To use Grants.gov, there are specific tasks that must be performed—some by the PI, and others by the institution. Getting to know Grants.gov means getting to know some of the intricacies of how the process works.

Know that registration with Grants.gov can take up to four weeks. If your institution is already registered, this is not a problem. Some colleges, universities, and nonprofits, however, have never submitted to Grants.gov and may not yet be registered. If your organization (or a partner) is not registered, it may not be possible to complete the registration process and prepare a proposal before the grant application deadline. It is better, therefore, to register for Grants.gov well before attempting to submit applications to federal competitions.

Appoint one person on the team as keeper of the application. Working with a Grants.gov application is challenging, especially the first time. If you are the PI and therefore doing most of the writing, get someone else on the team to prepare the application.

Know that a Grants.gov application is submitted in stages. On initial submission, the application is checked over by the Grants.gov system; if it passes this inspection, it will be passed on to the granting agency. It is possible to submit successfully to Grants.gov and have the submission returned by the agency for changes. Normally, these changes must be made and the application resubmitted before the deadline—another good reason to make the submission three days early!

Remember that errors and warnings happen. During the multistage submission process, you may receive error and warning messages from both Grants.gov and from the agency. Errors are mistakes in the application and must be corrected to complete the submission. Warnings do not stop the submission; however, they can result in disqualification if not amended. Investigate and resolve errors and warnings promptly and carefully.

Be ready to respond to the submission process of the agency. Different agencies have different procedures. Some simply take the application and respond six months later. Others may require approval by the authorized organization representative (AOR). If you are asked to take action by the agency, act promptly.

Box 8.3 The Nuts & Bolts: Grants.gov and NSF FastLane

The National Science Foundation (NSF) offers applicants the option of submitting via Grants.gov or via FastLane, the NSF-developed submission system. FastLane is considered an excellent online portal, and since it was designed to accommodate only NSF proposals, it is tailored to the documents and information required. FastLane does not have any catches or idiosyncratic processes. Most PIs and grants administrators prefer it to Grants.gov and use it when they can.

PREPARING A PROPOSAL FOR ONLINE SUBMISSION

Most online grant proposals are submitted in one of three ways: via email, as online documents, or in fields embedded in an online application. When submitting by email or uploading documents, the proposal is prepared very traditionally, as discussed in Chapter 7. After preparing the documents in a word processing program, you will convert them to PDFs and attach them to an email or upload them to a website or application (as with Grants.gov).

The writing, in this case, generally follows the same rules as traditional grant writing. You must pay attention to how the document looks after conversion and how "heavy" it is—very large documents may not be uploadable to government websites. Some submission portals (NSF FastLane, for example) may allow the upload of Word documents, but it is always better to perform your own conversions to PDF so that you know exactly what you are submitting. With good grant writing skills and some knowledge of a few software programs, most people can submit a grant proposal using these systems.

On the other hand, some online submission portals treat the proposal or letter of interest (LOI) like an application form, breaking down the component parts into fields. Submitting on such portals is more challenging for two reasons.

The creators of the application may have broken the proposal into non-traditional sections. When faced with application fields with unfamiliar questions or prompts, ask yourself, what is really being asked for? What would be the most straightforward answer? Keep in mind that the basic components of grants as discussed in this book (and others) are fairly universal, so if you are confused, try to associate an unfamiliar field with a standard proposal section. If you cannot figure it out, call the funder.

Online grant submission fields are generally very short. You must be able to write in a direct and concise manner, which can be quite challenging. Consider the character limits and develop short replies in a word processing document. When drafting your responses, it might be a good idea to make a list of the three most important ideas that must be conveyed, then work to write them as concisely as possible.

When writing concisely in short fields, style can be somewhat more informal. For example, I will probably use numerals rather than spelling out numbers (1 vs. one). I may try to do without adverbs, articles, and adjectives when possible. I will also favor the use of acronyms.

THE TOP 10 ONLINE SUBMISSION HAZARDS

1. Offline Items May Be Required

Both government agencies and foundations may solicit "mixed" applications, requiring both an online component and a postal component.

There is a foundation, for example, that requires one mailed copy of the application form and required attachments and four printed copies of the application form only—in addition to a very thorough online application. Note the differences in the number of copies required; this is not necessarily a straightforward task. In the middle of what appears to be strictly an online submission, the busy PI can overlook a relatively complex paper requirement.

Sometimes, even completely online federal submissions may be subject to Executive Order #12372, which requires the PI to fax or email a copy of the grant coversheet to the state office in charge of grant review.[1] Remember to check for hard copy requirements for online submissions.

> ### Box 8.4 The Nuts & Bolts:
> ### The More Directions the Better
>
> Although a large volume of directions can seem daunting, boring, impossible, and a waste of time, this "problem" is actually a blessing when submitting to Grants.gov. Why? Because each agency uses Grants.gov differently and has different interpretations and preferences for submissions. If the funder does not give you, the applicant, adequate instructions, you will never know what these preferences are. As a result, you may miss awards because of lack of compliance.
>
> When the agency is clear, meaning it provides adequate directions for using the package, you can feel secure that as long as you follow the directions, your proposal will be read and therefore considered for funding.

2. Submission Information May Be Located in Many Places

Guidelines may be available in multiple places, including on the grant application form itself. This means that as you are working through the guidelines, getting ready to copy and paste into the online form, you may suddenly find new directions five pages into the form! It is very important, therefore, to read everything before you begin preparing materials, including every page of the online form.

For proposals submitted through Grants.gov, guidelines may be available in at least four places: in the RFP from the agency, on the agency website, in the Grants.gov help files, and within the application itself. Foundation guidelines can also be found in a variety of places, including different pages of the website.

---

[1] If your submission is subject to this requirement, the information needed to comply will be available in the proposal guidelines.

3. Guidelines and Form Directions May Not Match

When a funder releases a separate set of guidelines and the online form, the PI should not assume that the documents are based on the same information. Each must be examined carefully. Application and guidance sections may be created by different teams at different times, perhaps for different purposes.

As you are reading the guidelines, take note of apparently repetitive sections in different documents. They may be offering different requirements. If the contradiction is problematic, contact the funder for guidance.

4. Fields Often Have Word and/or Character Limits

Many application fields will have character limits, which can be tricky. Not only do spaces and punctuation often count as characters, but the online application may also count them differently than your word processor does, resulting in diverse results when cutting and pasting pre-prepared contents to fields. The wise PI will give herself time to cut and paste responses to the online application in order to deal with potential issues that may arise.

5. Formatting Can Be a Challenge

Text fields often convert whatever is typed into them into a uniform format, regardless of any fonts, tables, bolding, headers, or other items the PI may desire to include. The contents of tables are particularly prone to showing up scrambled on the other end of an online application. In addition, some fields will reflect the formatting you type in; however, once the application is submitted, this formatting will not carry through in the final submission. In other words, you may add in the formatting, but the reviewers may not see it.

If possible, view the proposal as it will be seen by the reviewers before you submit. This can often be accomplished on the last screen just before the submit button, in a link labeled something like "Review Application" or "Print Application."

6. You Must Have an Adequate Computer and Software

Online submissions obviously require access to the Internet, and a reliable, speedy connection works best. If the machine takes more than a few seconds to load each page, the application preparation process can become onerous and time-consuming—a PI can even be timed out of the application if things are moving too slowly, and work can be lost.

There are other technical considerations as well. Final documents may be required to be submitted as PDFs. This necessitates access to Adobe Reader (a free download), at least, and possibly Adobe Acrobat. During submission, a computer may need to support at least five to six windows or programs open at a time, as the PI may be working between a word processing program, a spreadsheet program, a PDF maker, the RFP, and the submission portal as well as any other necessary programs.

7. Technical Difficulties Will Occur

Aside from any problems presented by the PI's computer, the online portal itself can present challenges. Mac users may experience challenges, and as with any Internet application, the website programming may not be easily accessed by the home system, even if it is a PC. It is therefore very important for the PI to give the application a test run well before the submission deadline to be sure that there are as few surprises as possible. This is yet another good reason to submit early.

8. You Should Get a Copy of the Submission

Once everything has been uploaded, edited, checked, and rechecked and you are just about ready to submit, acquire a full copy of the proposal. Many online applications will offer this option, located right next to the submit button or as part of the submission process. The result is often a PDF copy of the entire document, including all fields and attachments. This is extremely valuable as it is the record of what has been submitted: each address, telephone number, name, and response field, not to mention the final narrative and the budget. This copy can be saved, and if the PI is contacted by the funder about the application, she will have it as a ready reference.

Very occasionally, there is no formal way to acquire a copy as part of the submission process, in which case one should move through the completed, unsubmitted application taking screen shots of each page. In this case, it is also wise to open up and print each document that has been uploaded, unless a careful list has already been made of which version of each document was included in the submission.

9. Remember to Retain Your Receipt

Most online applications will include a receipt screen after submission is complete and/or send a receipt email to the PI. This screen or message may include an application number, or in the case of Grants.gov, a tracking number as well as the date and time of submission. It is very important to print a copy of both of these documents, perhaps as PDFs, and store them where they can easily be found again. The agency may require that application or tracking numbers be used in later correspondence about the proposal, whether in the event of funding or in the event of a problem with the proposal package. Additionally, it may be important to prove that the proposal was submitted within the deadline window. A receipt will do this.

When a proposal is submitted by email, a receipt is perhaps even more important. In these cases, the submission email should include a message requesting the favor of a reply to serve as a receipt. It is also important to retain the sent version of the message or to BCC oneself.

10. The Deadline May Be Measured in Hours

With hard copy submissions the proposal generally needs to arrive on a certain day, but for online submissions even the hour becomes important. Is it by the end of business that day? What time is that: Five o'clock? Six o'clock? If the funder is located in a different time zone, the applicant may be expected to convert this time to local time, so a 5 p.m. deadline in Washington, D.C., is actually a 2 p.m. deadline on the West Coast and even earlier in Hawaii.

Of course, if you submit three days early, these considerations become significantly less relevant.

THE NUTS & BOLTS

1. Although most grant applications are submitted online, some have offline elements—for example, documents that must be printed and submitted separately by post or fax.

2. There are three types of online submissions: emailed proposals, proposals uploaded to an electronic document, and online application forms.

3. Grants.gov is the main portal for searching and submitting federal grants.

4. Submitting many online proposals will require short and concise writing skills.

5. Allow yourself a minimum of three days to submit an online application. This will allow time to deal with the errors and glitches that are so common to online submissions.

EXERCISES: WORKING TOWARD MASTERY

Use the outline you created in Chapter 7 to write a 10-page proposal to a funder of your choice (plus budget and budget narrative). Refer to the following rubric as you create your outline.

Be sure to include the following:

1. A Fundable Idea (10 points): Build your proposal around an idea that is original, useful, and possible.

2. Research Questions/Goals (10 points): Present a clear statement of the research questions and/or goals. Label this section clearly.

3. Executive Summary/Abstract (10 points): Present a short but clear conceptualization of the project. Write this in a persuasive way that makes the reader want to know more about your project.

4. Literature Review/Background/The Case (10 points): Create a focused review of the relevant literature or a convincing account of the problem addressed by the project.

5. Project Description (10 points): Describe the project clearly. Carefully include what will happen, when, and the main work processes.

6. Evaluation (10 points): Present an evaluation plan that will inform you on project progress. How will you know whether the project is successful or not? How will you track progress? How will you know whether participants have been well served?

7. Conclusion (10 points): End the proposal formally. Summarize the project, re-present the most convincing points, discuss dissemination, or find another inventive way to end the proposal.

8. Budget and Budget Narrative (20 points): Present a reasonable budget that reflects the project description. Label the lines clearly. Make sure the numbers add up. Justify each line in terms of its function and how the cost was arrived at.

BONUS (10 points): Respond to an actual RFP or set of guidelines.

Notes: Methodology is not included here because there is no similar area to respond to when writing for a community service grant.

9

Polishing and Formatting the Proposal

INTRODUCTION

It is not quite enough to write a good proposal. One needs also to check for clarity, format the proposal, and clean up the text a bit. What follows are suggestions and steps that you can take before submission to present a more polished text. This chapter has a little grammar, a little graphic design, and a checklist for submission. I hope it helps you when you find yourself in that last rush before the deadline. That is the time when we are all most likely to forget things.

EDITING AND REVISING FOR CLARITY

Even the best writer will occasionally produce a sentence or two that does not make much sense. Great writers often work with great editors as close partners, and many successful grants are a product of both efforts. Over my time in the grants world, I have never seen an unedited proposal that could not benefit from some outside help. That is the nature of writing.

Academic writing suffers from a few common problems in terms of clarity. While there are many fine grammatical resources available to the PI and grant writer who need to review their skills, there are also a few tips I can share that most people can implement immediately to help their proposals shine.

I have found that three basic techniques can clean up many unclear sentences in academic grant writing:

1. Reorganize convoluted sentences
2. Use verb tenses effectively
3. Be aware of voice

Reorganize Convoluted Sentences

When editing academic writing, it is common to run into sentences that sound very intelligent but do not actually make sense. Because of the agglutinative nature of academic writing, the writer is tempted to add more and more clauses in an effort to be specific. Eventually the writer (and certainly the reader) may lose track of the subject and object of the sentence from within the many clauses.

Look at the following example:

Of course, external funding is not the whole story in terms of university quality; however, it is a useful rough index that can be far more easily employed in statistical analysis than the subjective rankings.

I wonder what this sentence is actually about: external funding or university quality? It sounds kind of smart, but it may not actually mean anything.

We will revise this sentence, but first let's review the subject-verb-object sentence construction in English:

I	ate	the Pop-Tart.
subject	verb	object

By definition, every complete sentence in English can be reduced to this structure. Sometimes the easiest place to start is with the verb. In fact, the convoluted sentence above has three verbs:

Of course, external funding is not the whole story in terms of university

                                  verb

quality; however, it is a useful rough index that can be far more easily

               verb   verb

employed in statistical analysis than the subjective rankings.

verb

After finding the verbs, I can spot the subjects fairly easily.

Of course, external funding is not the whole story in terms of university

subject   verb

quality; however, it (external funding) is a useful rough index that can be far

subject   verb   verb

more easily employed in statistical analysis than the subjective rankings.

verb

I begin to see the areas of confusion. Does the writer mean to say that external funding "is not the whole story in terms of university quality?" This can certainly be worded with more clarity.

Of course, external funding is not an adequate measure of university quality;

subject   verb

however, it (external funding) is a useful rough index that can be far more

subject   verb   verb

easily employed in statistical analysis than the subjective rankings.

That is better—the first line is making more sense. Next, there is a comparison going on in the second part of the sentence, that external funding is used in statistics more easily than *subjective rankings*, which are not defined. I wonder whether we even need *subjective rankings* in this sentence.

Of course, external funding is not an adequate measure of university quality;

subject   verb

however, it (external funding) is a useful rough index that can be

subject   verb   verb

easily employed in statistical analysis.

This sentence is getting better. My last question is whether the subject is clear enough. Does external funding mean philanthropy? Does it mean grants? I check the context of the sentence—it refers to research grants awarded across the university.

~~Of course,~~ While <u>total</u> external <u>research</u> funding alone is not an adequate measure of university quality, ~~however,~~ it is a useful rough index that can be easily employed in statistical analysis. ~~statistical techniques.~~

And what I like the best is that I have cut three words from this sentence, decreasing my word count just a bit.

While total external research funding alone is not an adequate measure of university quality, it is a useful rough index that can be easily employed in statistical analysis.

Use Verb Tenses Effectively

Use verb tenses in accordance with common sense. Things that happened in the past, including research cited from other authors, should be presented in the past tense, as simply as possible.

Abraham Wald introduced the Wald test of statistical parameters, an alternative to the likelihood ratio test.

When discussing an actual text, however, use the present tense.

Abraham Wald introduced the Wald test of statistical parameters, an alternative to the likelihood ratio test. He also wrote *Calculation and Elimination of Seasonal Fluctuations* in which he makes several significant arguments.

Use the present or future tense for your work or plans.

The PI, John Smith, serves as the Director of the Center for Political Economics.

The project team will assemble respondent names on a list for randomization.

Be Aware of Voice

Countless books on grant writing instruct the writer to avoid passive voice, and this is good advice. A sentence in active voice begins with the subject and is generally more direct and dynamic. A sentence in passive voice begins with the object; it is an inversion of sentence structure and is often an awkward construction.

When writing in active voice, you may choose the first-person or third-person point of view. First person is obviously the more dynamic choice, and it can be used in some disciplines and with some funders. However, there is an element of modesty in avoiding the strong first person (the use of the singular *I*). In practice, first person for the team is most often the softer *we*. If you can put your grant in first-person plural using *we*, I advise you to do so.

First-Person Active Voice

We will prepare and mail surveys to 1,000 Democratic and 1,000 Republican voters as well as 1,000 independents (1,000 + 1,000 + 1,000 = 3,000) from the Ann Arbor area in Fall 2013. **Surveys will include a link** to the project website for online data collection as well as a self-addressed and stamped return envelope for the convenience of the participants. **We will hire three undergraduate students** to perform data input for surveys that are mailed back.

First person helps keep the basic active sentence construction, subject-verb-object, up front and clear, which helps maintain clarity of expression. Use of third person in sentence two introduces some variation, and sentence three goes back to the first-person plural subject.

If first person is not appropriate for your project, consider using third-person active voice.

Third-Person Active Voice

The PI and her team will prepare and mail a total of 3,000 surveys: 1,000 Democratic and 1,000 Republican voters, as well as 1,000 independents (1,000 + 1,000 + 1,000 = 3,000) from the Ann Arbor area in Fall 2013. **The surveys will include a link** to the project website for online data collection as well as a self-addressed and stamped return envelope for the convenience of the participants. In addition, **three undergraduate students will be hired** to perform data input for surveys that are mailed back.

In this example third person is easy to use in sentence one (the PI and her team), which maintains the active voice. Sentence two features the third person with an object as the subject, and sentence three uses passive voice. In this case, use of passive voice at the end of a strong paragraph where the subject is understood keeps the information flowing and offers a varied sentence structure.

Using too many sentences with passive voice can deaden the proposal, however. Be sure to keep the active PI and team foremost in the reviewers' minds by using them as the subject regularly.

ACRONYMS

Acronyms or words formed from the initial letters of a title or phrase are a bane of grant writing. They are particularly problematic in connection with government grants, because the funders themselves use acronyms a great deal and the practice tends to spread to others in the grants community.

The heavy use of acronyms in grant writing can be like using a secret code that the reviewer does not understand. As such, acronyms can prevent comprehension of the proposal, and of course, an incomprehensible proposal is a poor outcome of the grant writing effort.

Here are a few tips for the appropriate use of acronyms:

Use acronyms that will be understandable to the reviewers. Unless you are certain of the discipline of the reviewers, do not use disciplinary acronyms. Many specific academic areas within disciplines have their own acronyms as well, and these should be avoided. On the other hand, using general, well-known acronyms is usually fine. For example, if you are submitting to the National Science Foundation, use of the acronym *NSF* is probably going to work for your proposal.

Spell out acronyms the first time they are used. Because of the cut-and-paste editing process, the placement of the first use of an acronym may change, causing it to be inadvertently undefined the first time it appears. Check for this after editing is completed and before submission.

Feel free to redefine acronyms. If you define an acronym on Page 2 and do not use it again until Page 6, consider redefining it for the reader, or better yet, spell the phrase out on each use.

When naming your project, consider using a shortened title rather than an acronym. Instead of creating a convoluted title to produce an appropriate acronym or using a meaningless acronym in place of your title, shorten the title. See the examples in the table below.

Full Title	Possible Name
The Community Economic Development Project	The Community Project
The University-High School STEM Alliance	The STEM Alliance
North-South Immigration Outcomes	North-South

Introduce few new acronyms. The average person can keep two to three new acronyms in mind while reading a complex text. Although it might affect your word count, spell acronyms out whenever it will help the reader. Clarity is the most important aspect of a well-written proposal.

FORMATTING: THE CREATION OF WHITE SPACE

Organization and readability are assisted by the use of structural formatting elements: white space, headings, bullets, and tables. For the reader, these elements may represent the difference between a pleasant, fluid reading experience and deciphering a monolithic block of text.

For example, which of the two pages in Figure 9.1 look like they would be easier to read?

Four Ways to Create White Space

White space is the absence of text, and it draws the reader's eye across a page. Here are four ways to preserve white space and help your pages look inviting and readable.

Make Headings Work for You

There are writers who do not like to use headings in their work because headings break the flow of the narrative. While this is somewhat true, using titles is strongly advised in grant writing for two reasons:

Figure 9.1   Two Examples of the Same Text

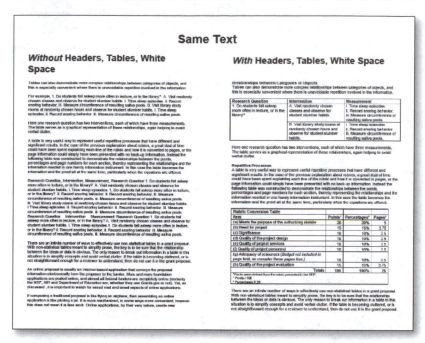

Notice how the eye is attracted to the white space on both pages and how the tables on the right page draw attention. The left page is readable, although because it does not organize ideas graphically, it may be more difficult to follow. This is not to say that compacted, cramped, no-white-space proposals do not get funded: they occasionally do, in spite of poor formatting.

1. *Clearly demarcated sections help the reviewer to follow arguments and check off rubrics.* Reviewers are often asked to assign scores to specific sections, so they need to refer to these sections quickly and easily as they work. Given this requirement, it is important that a reviewer is not forced to estimate or, worse, to guess the location of a required section because of an absence of headings. Helping the reviewer to know exactly where the required sections are can only help your score.

2. *Forming transitions between major narrative sections can be difficult.* In the midst of finishing a narrative on deadline, it will be challenging to sculpt transitions between unrelated sections. Headings avoid this, saving time and effort.

All sections should be clearly labeled with consistent headings, much as the sections and subsections of this book are. Short and simple bolded items work well. Italicized text must be easy to read or it should not be used in headings.

It is possible to use a different font for the headings if it works well with the main body font, although this can make formatting a more complex task. If using a distinct heading font, be sure that the funder allows it and that the reviewer will not see it as garish. For most proposals, it is pointless to use a larger font for titles; in the end, one is always scrambling for more space, and those headers will inevitably be decreased in size to make room for sparkling narrative. I tend to use bolded text for all headings in my grant proposals.

Recognize the Power of Bullets and Lists

Smart grant writers use bulleted lists to help readers find information quickly and create more white space. Numbers should be used instead of bullet points for lists that are arranged in an order of significance or that will be referred to within the text.

Notice how much more readable the information below is when presented as a list:

In grant writing, one must be aware of several important points, listed in order of significance: writing structure, formal wording, budgets, evaluation, methodology, and a few basic legal concepts.

In grant writing, one must be aware of the following:

1. Writing structure

2. Formal wording

3. Budgets

4. Evaluation

5. Methodology

6. A few basic legal concepts

When using bullets, decide on the bullet style and keep to it. Unobtrusive looking bullets are most welcome.

Be careful not to create excessively long lists; five to seven items is plenty. Most word processing programs make bulleted lists extremely easy: PIs who find themselves manually spacing to get a neat set of bulleted lists are not obtaining the full benefit of their software. Click "help" and search for "bulleted lists" to get instructions.

Create Tables

While tables are very often employed to present statistical analysis, they are also a useful method to convey other types of information in a graphic, easy to understand manner. Tables can be used to convey bits of information in the proposal in a way that can save time, space, and frustration. The key is finding conceptual ways to relate the information and employing this in the table design. Some basic concepts that can be easily presented in tables include the following:

- Simple one-to-one relationships
- Relationships between classes of objects
- Repetitive processes

Tables and Simple One-to-One Relationships. A table can present simple relationships systematically and without verbal clutter. For example, if in this book I want to present the idea behind each section of the traditional proposal, I can express in prose:

> The Executive Summary/Abstract presents an answer to the question, "What is this project basically about?" and the Case/Background/Literature Review must present information that answers the question, "Why is it important?" The Project Description has the job to present what will actually happen if the project is funded, while the Methodology answers the question, "How will it be done?" "How will it be measured?" belongs in the Evaluation section, and then we end with a Call to Action in the Conclusion.

The table presenting this information is shorter and easier to understand; it also cuts the verbal clutter.

1. Executive Summary/Abstract	What is this project basically about?
2. The Case/Background/Literature Review	Why is it important?
3. Project Description	What will actually happen?
4. Methodology	How will it be done?
5. Evaluation	How will it be measured?
6. Conclusion	Why should we fund it?

Tables and Relationships Between Categories of Objects. Tables can also demonstrate more complex relationships between categories of objects, and this is especially convenient when your information involves unavoidable repetition.

Research Question	Intervention	Measurement
Do students fall asleep more often in lecture or in the library?	A. Visit randomly chosen classes and observe for student slumber habits.	i. Time sleep episodes. ii. Record snoring behavior. iii. Measure circumference of resulting saliva pools.
	B. Visit library study rooms at randomly chosen hours and observe for student slumber habits.	i. Time sleep episodes. ii. Record snoring behavior. iii. Measure circumference of resulting saliva pools.

Here one research question has two interventions, each of which has three measurements. The table serves as a graphical representation of these relationships, again helping to avoid verbal clutter.

Tables and Repetitive Processes. A table is a very useful way to represent repetitive processes. In the previous discussion of rubrics, a great deal of time could have been spent explaining each line of the rubric and how it is converted to pages. Instead, the following table demonstrates the relationships between the points and presents the percentages and page numbers for each section, all in one handy information instrument. There is an element of elegance to this sort of table when it is well executed.

Rubric Conversion Table			
Item	Points[1]	Percentages[2]	Pages[3]
(a) Meets the purpose of the authorizing statute	20	20%	5
(b) Need for project	15	15%	3.75

Rubric Conversion Table			
Item	Points[1]	Percentages[2]	Pages[3]
(c) Significance	10	10%	2.5
(d) Quality of the project design	10	10%	2.5
(e) Quality of project services	10	10%	2.5
(f) Quality of project personnel	10	10%	2.5
(g) Adequacy of resources *(The budget is not included in page limit, so consider these pages free.)*	10	10%	2.5
(h) Quality of the project evaluation	15	15%	3.75
Totals	**100**	**100%**	**25**

[1] Points were derived from the rubric presented in the RFP.

[2] Points/100

[3] Percentages × 25

Include Images

Images add white space and inform the project description by providing valuable context. Although one should avoid including irrelevant or decorative images, judiciously selected, informative pictures can greatly assist the reviewers' grasp of the project.

There are a few issues to consider when including images with a proposal:

- **Be sure the image is legible.** Black and white images require relatively high contrast in order to be easily seen. Images should be crisp, not blurry. Additionally, color images may be printed out on paper in black and white during the review process, so print color images in black and white before inclusion to check for contrast.
- **Images should capture the most important ideas you want to present.** Be sure that the figure or scene is complete and of an adequate size

in relation to the total size of the image. Cropping and resizing can help focus attention on aspects of the figures you want to emphasize.

- **Color images inflate file size**, although technology is changing and it is becoming easier to include color images with a proposal. This will depend on the size of the image (in bytes or kilobytes) in relation to the number of bytes or kilobytes allowed by the submission portal. Image size and quality can be adjusted in various image manipulation programs.
- **Images look very different on a computer screen than they do on the printed page.** Even if you submit the proposal online, the reviewers may print it out for consideration, so be sure to print out the completed proposal with images before you submit it. Not only will the images look different, but the placement of the images on the page may shift with printing.

Always provide captions for your images, because you are using them to communicate specific ideas. As with writing the proposal, do not assume that readers will automatically understand the ideas that you are trying to convey.

MAKING YOUR PROPOSAL FIT

There will come a moment in grant preparation when you have written the proposal, the budget is done, and the submission is authorized. It is common at this point to realize that you are three pages over the maximum number of pages that will be accepted by the funder. Now you must work to make the grant fit in the space you have available.

My first strong recommendation is:

DO NOT CUT THE WHITE SPACE!

It will be the first thing you want to do, but do not cut white space unless you are quite desperate. There are many other ways that a proposal can be shortened besides making it an unreadable block of text.

Edit Out Repetitious and Useless Text

Read the text carefully, and read it out loud if possible. Question whether each idea carries water or provides important information for your proposal. Can a four-paragraph discussion be cut to three? Are there unnecessary sentences? I usually begin with sections and paragraphs, work my way down to sentences, and then begin cutting phrases and words. I always cut enough of a paragraph to eliminate the few words left on a line by themselves at the end of it (called "orphans" by some). It is a wonderful opportunity to get a full line of space by cutting only two or three words.

Work With Line Spacing and Margins

You might be tempted to manipulate line spacing and margins to save space (if the funder's guidelines allow flexibility with these). Try very hard not to do this. First make every attempt to cut your proposal by streamlining the writing, cutting unnecessary clauses, and modifying your ideas. Altering spacing and margins requires that you sacrifice white space.

There are funders who are liberal on the matter of margins, allowing them to be set as small as .5 inches; however, having permission to use narrow margins does not mean it is a good idea. One-inch margins are recommended. If these need to be (and are allowed to be) altered, then narrow all four margins at the same time in tenths of an inch. For example, use .9 inches all around rather than .5 inches for the left and right and 1 inch for the top and bottom. Narrowing in equal measure all around the page keeps the space balanced and narrows only to what is needed, thereby preserving as much white space as possible.

Similarly, follow the funder's direction for line spacing and do not adjust the line spacing to less than single spaced. If the text is already single spaced, preserve a line of space between each paragraph, even when using paragraph indents. Insert a line of space between images and tables and the text. If you must alter the text spacing, I advise the diminishment of lines between paragraphs by about a tenth of a point until the desired size is achieved. In other words, you can use a 12-point font and 8-point spaces between paragraphs.

Box 9.1   Follow Directions

Follow directions. Follow directions.
    . . . and when in doubt, follow directions!

Alter Text Spacing, Font, and Headers

Text spacing is how close the letters are to one another. Avoid overcompacting the letters, as this creates true congestion in the text:

This sentence is spaced normally at 11 points.

This sentence is condensed at .1 point.

This sentence is condensed at .5 points.

A .1-point condensation throughout the text will hardly be noticed and can conserve real space. A few funders specify how many characters must fit into a specific amount of space to guard against extreme compaction of letters, however.

In most cases the font and font size are dictated by the funder. When they are not, keep it simple and easy to read. Times New Roman (TNR) is always a good choice and is actually quite a compacted, space-saving font. If your reviewers will be reading from a computer screen (this is more and more common), you may choose a sans serif font like Arial. Verdana and Garamond, two popular alternate choices, are rather broad, taking up more space per word, so they are not recommended.

When absolutely necessary, the headers can be made smaller. They can also be placed on the same line with the sentences that follow. For example:

Project Description: This project is going to make things much better in our community . . .

After cutting the text, it is better to use all of these strategies in small amounts all at the same time. That way you will create space without drawing attention to the process while preserving all the white space possible.

LAST CALL: THINGS TO CHECK BEFORE SUBMISSION

After everything seems finished, it is important to make a few last checks. These are the things that will give your proposal a finished quality.

Master List Check. Whenever I begin working on a submission, one of my first steps is to create a master list of every item that is required for a successful submission, along with every related task. I create this on the basis of the RFP or guidelines and on the basis of my institutional requirements. I check these items off, one by one, as I get them done, then just before submission I double check the list. Create your own task list when you begin a project and be sure to include the things you tend to forget. It will be a lifeline for you during the pressure of submission.

Spelling and Punctuation Check. Everyone knows that spelling, punctuation, and grammar are important, but this is easy to forget when you are focused on how to make complex ideas understandable for your audience or when you are in the middle of the submission rush. I know that you know how to spell receive (not recieve), but the reviewers do not. Frankly, some reviewers will assume that your spelling errors are NOT typos or inadvertent mistakes. The reviewers may assume that these reflect a lack of education, understanding, or professionalism. It is not a kind assumption, but it is made regularly, so run spell check and pay attention to grammar, usage, and other details.

I run spell check on the last draft of the proposal because otherwise I would be running it every time someone works on the text. When I run spell check on a submission, the train is just about to leave the station, meaning I am just about to submit.

Citation Check. Citations are another detail that can be overlooked while creating a great proposal, and errors will reflect badly on the PI. Even if you are using OneNote, print out your reference list and read it. Is it alphabetized properly? Do you have all the identifying elements for each reference? Is everything that must be capitalized, capitalized? Is everything that must be italicized, italicized? Does every item that appears on the reference list appear as a citation and vice versa? Most competitions will not dictate which citation style to use; so, choose one and stick with it throughout the proposal.

Widow and Orphan Check. Check your document for sentences that appear to be separated from their paragraphs. Sometimes the first line of a paragraph is left on the previous page (a widow); other times, the last line of the paragraph is presented on the subsequent page (an orphan). Sometimes you have just a word or two of text at the end of a paragraph taking up an entire line. Add spaces or delete material to make content fit better. Some software programs are better at preventing widows and orphans than others, but nothing can replace the PI's careful attention.

Tables and Illustrations Check. While checking for widows and orphans, check to be sure that all of your tables, charts, and illustrations are still in the proposal, where you want them, and uncompromised by the various changes the editing process may have subjected them to.

Headings Check. Are your headings the size you set for them and the style you set for them? Particularly if the document has been handed around to different team members, old code can show up at inopportune times, meaning that suddenly, as you get ready to submit, a heading will change to a different font or a different size (or even a different language). Rather than struggling with the (invisible) code, I suggest you clear the formatting before you bring it into line with the rest of the text.

Spacing Check. Print the proposal out and go over it one more time to check on spacing between all elements. Nothing beats a printed proposal to help you find errors.

WORKING WITH YOUR SPONSORED PROJECTS OFFICE

The majority of the writing described in this chapter involves editing, proofreading, and formatting. Lucky PIs have sponsored projects staff members who can and are willing to review their narratives. Many times, however, sponsored projects staff specialize in financial issues and/or are already quite overworked, so they may not be able to offer this type of support. They may know a few editors that they can recommend, however, if this is needed.

THE NUTS & BOLTS

1. Be aware of the danger of long, complex academic sentences that do not make sense. When you find them, break them down into their component parts to fix them.

2. Use the most active voice you can in the proposal writing.

3. Use white space in your proposal to help the reader's eye move across the text. When you begin cutting your narrative, try very hard NOT to cut your white space.

4. When cutting the proposal, work on making your text concise before altering the formatting. If you must cut with formatting changes, use several different techniques in small ways so the cutting is not obvious to the reviewer.

5. Before you submit, check your materials carefully: Do you have everything required? Have you spell checked? Are your citations in good shape? Do not forget to check on widows and orphans, headings, tables, and illustrations.

EXERCISES: WORKING TOWARD MASTERY

If you are reading this book as part of a class, exchange the proposal you developed for Chapter 8 with a classmate. Take the other person's proposal home and read it carefully. Consider it from a reviewer's perspective. What is being proposed? How clear is the proposal about what will actually take place if this project is funded?

Use the rubric below to rate this proposal. Include comments that highlight both the good things your classmate has accomplished with this work as well as the areas in need of improvement. Remember that you are helping your classmate to create a better proposal, so include one suggestion for each criticism.

While it is entirely appropriate to deduct points for spelling, grammar, and style, this should NOT be the main point of the critique. Address the questions in each rubric area.

Rubric

1. A Fundable Idea (10 points): Does this proposal present an idea that is original, useful, and possible?

2. Research Questions/Goals (10 points): Does the proposal present a clear statement of research questions and/or goals? Is this section clearly labeled?

3. Executive Summary/Abstract (10 points): Is this a short but clear conceptualization of the project? Does it make you want to read more?

4. Literature Review/Background/The Case (10 points): Has the author provided a focused review of the relevant literature, or has she or he presented a convincing account of the problem addressed?

5. Project Description (10 points): Has the project been adequately described? Can you understand what will happen and when? Are the main work processes clear?

6. Methodology (if included) (10 points): Is the research process clear? Does this section include information about the investigative process, data gathering, data storage, and analysis?

7. Evaluation (if included) (10 points): Does the PI present an evaluation plan? Is it clear how he or she will know whether the project is successful?

8. Conclusion (10 points): How does the proposal end? Is this an effective ending that tells you more about the project or highlights important aspects of it?

9. Budget and Budget Narrative (20 points): Does the budget appear reasonable? Does it reflect the project description? Are the lines clearly labeled? Do the numbers add up? Is each line justified in terms of its function and how the cost was arrived at?

BONUS (10 points): Does the proposal respond adequately to a real RFP or set of guidelines?

If you are reading this book on your own, ask a colleague (especially a colleague with grants experience) to edit your proposal. Have this person use the rubric above to rate your proposal and then explain his suggestions to you.

Resist the urge to argue when you do not agree; rather, be open to all of your colleagues' ideas and then adjust your proposal accordingly. This is good practice for receiving reviewers' comments from funding agencies!

10

Declines, Awards, and Grant Administration

Grant proposals have two outcomes: They are either awarded or not awarded. This is a simple yet stressful reality for the PI, and the fear of being declined deters many from applying for grants.

Successful grant seekers, however, are turned down all the time. They may even be turned down more than other grant seekers because they tend to apply more often. Let me repeat that—successful grant seekers tend to be turned down more often than unsuccessful grant seekers because they submit more grant proposals.

Why would a person persevere against the odds of decline and submit even more proposals? There are at least four good reasons:

1. **The PI knows the odds.**

   She knows that the more she submits, the more chances she has to be awarded.

2. **Experience in submission is the best builder of grant writing skill.**

   This is true even when the submission is declined.

3. **The more feedback the PI gets, the better.**

   The more comments you can get from reviewers, the more skilled you can become at developing your proposals to address specific funder interests and concerns.

4. Funding trends shift.
Today's rejected idea might be awarded tomorrow.

Obviously, no one likes to be declined. No one ever gets used to it. It is naturally unpleasant and can feel very personal. Declines have an important part to play in developing grant writing skills, though. If you pay attention to reviewer comments and continue to build your skills, your chances of an award will continue to grow through each decline.

DECLINES

A decline is a message, often an email, from the funder informing the applicant that a submission has not been approved for funding. A decline may come soon after the submission, or it may come at the same time the award notifications are sent out.

Many people think that the later they hear from the funder, the more likely it is that they are going to be awarded. This is to some extent true: Early messages from the funder are often declines. Some funders, however, send notices, awards, and declines out to all applicants at the same time, so assuming that a late notice is an award notification can lead to disappointment.

The way that people deal with declines has a great deal to do with their expectations. If they expect to be awarded, a decline can be difficult to receive. If they are realistic about the odds and work to keep the situation impersonal, then a decline may be disappointing but not tragic. The fact is, many excellent proposals—based on good ideas, and written well and according to directions—get turned down. When agencies get to the end of their budgets, they must stop awarding, even when they still have worthy applications.

A decline, therefore, can mean many things:

- A decline may first and foremost mean that the submission was not completed properly.
- The funder was not ready for the idea.
- The idea was not communicated clearly.
- The funder ran out of money set aside for this competition.
- The funder does not know you, the applicant, well enough yet.
- The funder is not familiar with your institution or organization.

This last point is very important. Certain colleges and universities may be very familiar to the funder and therefore favored for funding. Many of these are the famous research universities spread across the United States.

Of course, there are many good schools, not all of them famous. If you work at a predominantly undergraduate institution (PUI) it may be a little harder to get the notice of a funder (whether a foundation or a government agency). Consider applying via special programs for predominantly undergraduate and under-awarded institutions. Both the National Science Foundation (NSF) and the National Institutes of Health (NIH), for example, have programs designed for such colleges and universities. Also consider enlisting the assistance of your school's corporate and foundation relations department to try to build a relationship with a specific foundation.

In any case, the next step after a decline is to work with reviewer comments in order to improve the next submission.

WORKING WITH REVIEWERS' COMMENTS

Research grant competitions are decided by a panel of reviewers, often faculty in the relevant discipline or a related field (although not always). Most federal competitions will send the reviewers' comments automatically with the decline letter. If your proposal is declined and you are sent the reviewer comments, study these to learn what you can do to make future submissions better.

If reviews are not included with the decline letter, it is a good idea to call the funder and request them. Some foundations may not make reviews available to declined applicants. In this case, you can call and ask for any information about how the proposal could have been made a better fit. Do this as soon as possible after receiving the decline, meaning after you have had a few days to adjust to the news but before the staff of the foundation forgets what happened during the review.

If you submit to a peer-reviewed competition and are declined without review, have your proposal looked at by a successful grant awardee and take notes. Generally if a proposal is not reviewed, there were serious problems.[1]

There are a few important points to keep in mind while working with reviewers' comments:

- **See comments as assistance, not criticism.** Reviewers are trying to help you improve future proposals. Of course, the reviews are more helpful when suggestions accompany the critique: Remember that someday when you become a reviewer! In the meantime, be patient and learn.

---

[1] The exception to this could be if the proposal was faulted on a technicality.

- **There are usually three or more reviewers.** Comments will therefore come from a variety of perspectives. This is an opportunity to see your proposal from different angles.
- **Not every comment is of equal value.** You may disagree with some on principle, and some may refer to ideas you already thought about and discarded—yet others will be insightful and important. Open your mind to everything your reviewers offer, and then put aside comments that are not helpful.
- **Important comments will often (although not always) be repeated by more than one reviewer.** Any suggestion that two or more reviewers agree on should certainly be addressed in revisions.
- **Sometimes the reviewers will miss aspects of your proposal.** If a reviewer notes that an important point was missing when it was, in fact, covered in the proposal, this indicates that the point needed to be made more clearly, repeated, or highlighted in some way. Many PIs see this situation as the "fault" of the reviewers, when this is far from the truth. If you did not make the point clear enough for reviewers to retain, then the writing is at fault and revision is necessary.

Hold on to the reviews and use them to rewrite the next submission, especially when applying to the same funder. Some funders will even have your subsequent submission reviewed by the same reviewers (the NIH may do this), in which case it is even more important to address reviewers' suggestions carefully. In many cases, you will be asked to attach a document detailing how the new proposal responds to the previous review.

Box 10.1   The Nuts & Bolts: When NOT to Call the Funder

Do not call the funder to inquire about why you were declined while you are feeling emotional, disappointed, or irritated. While your feelings are certainly valid, showing them may not reflect well on you as a PI. Remember that every contact with the funder is an opportunity to build a relationship, so make all contact as positive and useful as possible.

Calling the funder a week after you receive the decline is soon enough. Just ask the staff member, "How could I have developed my proposal in a way that would have better met the reviewers' expectations?"

AWARDS

Awards are far more fun to receive, of course. When you are awarded, it means your project has been validated through competition and found excellent. Someone believes so strongly in your idea that they have sent or will shortly send money to see the project accomplished. This feeling of gratification is hard to beat and is, frankly, a bit addictive—sustained grant seeking is no mystery to those who have experienced the thrill of being awarded.

Even awards can be tricky, however. First of all, remember that a funder may engage in what appears to be encouraging communication—telephone calls, emails, personal conversations—yet not ultimately award funding to you. A program officer can be very friendly and encouraging, but that does not necessarily mean an award is imminent. An award is not made until an award letter is received. In some cases, the award is not made until your institution signs a contract and the agency countersigns it.

Awards can also be complicated because often the initial notice of an award is really the beginning of a negotiation. Although it is possible to write a proposal for $50,000 and receive a check in the mail for $50,000, you are also likely to receive an email award that requests you cut 15 percent from the budget and add an evaluation.

Many faculty PIs do not realize that the award letter often represents the beginning of a negotiation. When an award letter is received, a university representative, usually a sponsored projects staff member, should be contacted immediately. Because the grant agreement is ultimately between the funder and the institution, institutional representatives may need to execute grant agreements, approve budget revisions, and generally be aware that an award is taking place. Sponsored projects, risk management, and even legal counsel may be involved in negotiating and accepting an award.

CONTENTS OF THE AWARD LETTER

A grant award is generally conveyed in a letter, which may or may not be accompanied by a check. The award letter often contains terms for the grant or rules that the PI and the university must follow during the funding period; for example, an award letter usually lists the due dates for reports and sometimes how the money can and cannot be spent. Some award letters are very brief and perfunctory. Others are voluminous, resemble contracts, and require an administrator's signature.

The award letter often reveals the very important award start date and end date. Grant expenses may not be honored by the funder until the start date. This means that the PI may be restricted from expending money on grant items before the start date, which means that pre-award expenses will not be reimbursed. In some cases the award may not begin until the contract is countersigned. In these cases the PI may experience a few weeks of uncertainty until funds are available.

The end date is the final day during which project activities can be funded through a specific grant. The end date marks the end of the project—unless an extension is granted. No charges can be applied to the grant after the end date has passed. The end date is often set simply, for example, three years after the start date, although it could be set by a variety of processes. The important thing is to keep this deadline in mind as you implement your grant.

The award terms may also include important daily considerations, such as, which grant reports are due when, whether public announcements of the grant must include reference to the funder, and how and under what circumstances the budget can be revised.

For example, some funders frown on rolling money over to the next year if one year is underspent, while other funders have no problem with this. Some funders allow money to be shifted from one budget line to another per the circumstantial needs of the project, and others want a revision submitted to a program officer any time 10 percent or more will be shifted between budget lines.

Many PIs feel that the grant is "their money" and, as responsible adults, they should be able to administer it as they see fit. This is an understandable sentiment, but grant awards are rarely structured this way. Good stewardship means following the funder's budget rules and the grant protocol of your institution.

Box 10.2 True Story

I once worked on a project with a PI who was so excited about a new award that he issued a press release shortly after receiving the award letter. Unfortunately, he had not completely read the award letter, and it contained two terms regarding award announcements:

1. The award was not to be announced until the signed

award letter was received back and acknowledged by the funder.

2. All communications regarding the award were to be approved by the program officer before release.

The grant was only three days old and we were already apologizing to the funder!

Of course, the PI called and explained, and in the end, the funder approved the press release. Everything went forward in a very positive manner—although technically the PI's error could have cost him the grant!

GOOD STEWARDSHIP

Merriam Webster defines stewardship in this way:

> The conducting, supervising, or managing of something; especially: the careful and responsible management of something entrusted to one's care. (2014)

A grant award is the entrustment of resources to the care of a PI and an institution so that a research or community service project may be conducted according to the plan presented by the grant proposal. Taking good care of grant money is called good stewardship. There are several aspects of stewardship related to grants.

A grant is expected to contribute toward a definite goal as defined in the proposal. Grant monies are therefore not given outright: They are in some sense shared between the funder, the institution, and the awardee until they are spent out for project expenses.

Progress toward this goal is generally documented by reports to the funder. Reports will be further discussed a little later in this chapter.

Care must be taken to spend grant funds as detailed in the budget and narrative. On the financial side, grant funds are often managed through specific account networks, and the funds are generally not commingled with other types of institution monies.

Expenditures must be documented with receipts. Whenever you, as an awarded PI, spend money on grant activities, you must acquire an itemized receipt in order to provide documentation. Your school will most likely require this, partly as a best practice of grants management and partly because the financial staff will be required to submit receipts if the grant is ever audited.

Communication with the funder must be maintained, especially when things go wrong. Even when the PI is paying careful attention to the budget and other administrative tasks, there will be times when the grant does not progress according to plan. Whether this calls for a budget revision (see below), an extension, or a new project plan, keep the funder in the loop. Be sure they understand what the problem is and most importantly, what you are doing to solve it.

In some cases, the context of the project is different from what you anticipated when you were putting the budget together. Perhaps unexpected needs have emerged. Perhaps the project must accomplish a goal in a different way. Whatever the reason, the current budget may be found ineffective for project needs. In this case, good stewardship requires that you engage the post-award analyst and the funder in conversations about revising the budget and perhaps the project. These conversations should lead to specific steps to structure the budget more effectively. Most funders and institutions will require that any new budget be submitted for approval.

Administering the Project

After all the documents have been signed, the funds are available for use, and the start date arrives, the project can begin. But how do you begin project activities in an institutional context?

Once an award has been made, the project moves into what is commonly called the post-award phase or, simply, post award. Staff assistance during this time most often comes in the form of a financial analyst who advises on and monitors spending. The analyst may work out of sponsored projects, the controller's office, or another university department. You may also find yourself working with human resources (HR), student services, financial aid, facilities, and so forth, depending on the specific project.

At some universities, sponsored projects schedules a "setup" meeting as soon as funds become available. During this meeting, the PI is introduced to grant financial processes and to the university personnel who will make up the grant implementation team.

Whatever your institutional setting, whether a department-level administrator handles award management or the central office does, there are several questions you may need to consider as you move into post award or implementation:

Which staff member(s) will be overseeing the grant accounts and in what capacity? How much assistance can you expect? At some institutions, the PI is encouraged to work actively with a financial analyst. She can ask questions, get reports on expenditures, and obtain assistance with budget revisions. At other institutions, the PI is essentially on her own. Knowing whether there is someone to help, gaining access to this person, and establishing a good working relationship are very important.

How does the PI actually spend funds out? In some institutions, a payment card can be issued for use of grant funds; at others, forms must be submitted in advance each and every time an expenditure is planned. Find out the correct way to make purchases and follow it. Every institution wants receipts, so plan on keeping those and submitting them to the analyst. If you as the PI really are on your own, be sure to retain all receipts, as the funder will most likely call upon you to document your expenses.

What happens if a budget line is overspent? At some schools this is impossible, because a financial analyst must oversee every purchase. At other schools all spending is in the PI's hands and overspending is a genuine possibility. Knowing the protocol at your school is critical and will prevent challenging situations, such as being told by the analyst that you cannot buy something or, worse, that you have already overspent your grant, yet still have many expenses waiting.

What are the procedures for grant hiring and for paying personnel? This process can take longer than you might expect. Many major grant administration problems have started out as seemingly minor delays in hiring or challenges getting students, vendors, or subcontractors paid. Know the forms, know the deadlines, know who to ask for help, and if needed, seek assistance early.

How is travel arranged? Is it as simple as taking the trip and turning in the receipts? Some institutions have specific preapproval processes, and others do not. Most institutions avoid per diems, providing reimbursement after the submission of receipts.

How are participant incentives paid? If you must provide incentives for research study participants, cover this process early. Many post-award offices resist providing envelopes of cash or gift cards to participants, as these can easily go unaccounted for. Discover your post-award office's protocol for providing incentives, and negotiate a procedure that works for your project.

What reports are required and when? Most funders require reports of various types, and even when they do not, it is good stewardship to provide them. The minimum is a financial and narrative report, provided one or two months after the project is concluded. At most universities, the post-award financial analyst issues the financial reports, but it is a good idea to check on this. Find out how much assistance will be provided by the analysts at your institution. For example, if they prepare the financial report, will they submit it to the funder as well? If you write the narrative report, will they submit that along with the financials?

The importance of maintaining close contact with the university staff members assigned to assist with your grant cannot be overemphasized. A good working relationship can help you avoid a great deal of hassle during the inevitable ups and downs of project management. Plan to touch base with your financial analyst at least every quarter, more preferably every month. Tell her how things are going, anticipate your major upcoming expenditures with her, and get a report on the progress of the grant spending. One simple 30-minute meeting each month can save a great deal of trouble over the life of the project.

Box 10.3   The Nuts & Bolts: Five Ways NOT to Spend a Grant

This chapter deals with very abstract concepts of stewardship: Only spend what you budgeted—no more, no less. Here are a few real-life examples of things PIs have tried to spend grant money on:

- One PI tried to pay a parking ticket with grant money because he was "on grant business" when he got it.
- Many PIs attempt to charge copy costs to their grants. Unless a specific grant copy code has been assigned through the institution (or the department), this is unallowable.
- Many PIs attempt to buy laptops for general use with their grants.
- Many PIs attempt to have a glass of wine on the grant while traveling.
- PIs may try to meet their colleagues for project discussions at posh resorts.

All of these types of spending are unallowable.

Pace Yourself: Spending the Grant Out

When you built your budget, you paced spending according to your projected needs. You estimated which resources would be necessary in year one, in year two, in year three, and so forth. Therefore, you should spend the money in that way. Buy the equipment that you planned to buy at the time you forecast the project. Do not buy more, and do not buy less.

Overspending the Grant

Overspending the grant is a very normal problem. It often occurs because a busy PI is grappling with many commitments and is not tracking spending. Perhaps conditions have changed and he needs a few things that he had not planned on, so he buys them. Rather than talking to the budget analyst, he simply moves forward.

Overspending the grant is problematic because once one budget line is overspent, there will be fewer resources available for the other lines, meaning that other needs may not be met. When funds need to be shifted from one line to another, this should be done thoughtfully, through budget revisions, and with the help of the budget analyst.

A badly overspent grant can result in the money running out before the project is complete. There are only two solutions to this problem, and neither is a good option:

1. **The project stops,** resulting in a default on the grant.

2. **More money must be found** to complete the project.

Pay attention to the budget throughout the project period. Be thoughtful about departures from the budget plan, and document these with the post-award analyst and, if necessary, the funder.

Underspending the Grant

There are also PIs who underspend their grants. Some of them are very busy and perhaps not paying attention to the budget. Others, however, attempt to "save" the money. They feel that by spending less money, they are demonstrating good stewardship.

There are many problems with underspent grants for all parties involved.

The funds may remain with the funder. This is true for most federal grants because federal agencies generally reimburse the institution for grant expenses. This means that if the money is never spent, the funds sit with the agency, and the university never receives them. As a matter of organizational management, badly underspent grants impact the funder as well because federal agencies need to spend out what they project in order to receive their next budget request properly.

The funds may need to be returned to the funder. Some foundations may award funds all at once, sending a check with the award letter. If the funds are not fully used, however, they also may require that the institution refund them. Universities do not like to send money back, and funders do not like to have their awards returned.

Underspent grants are thought to reflect poor budgeting skills and management. As such, they do not reflect well on the PI or the institution. Be straightforward with your grants: Budget what you need, and use what you budget.

Underspent grants may indicate that the project was not conducted fully. If, in the initial proposal, specific items were requested to get the work done, the assumption is that those items were required for successful project completion.

If conditions change, of course, this should be communicated to the funder early, and an alternative plan should be prepared. Perhaps the goals of the grant could be enlarged in some way; for example, a larger number of participants could be served with the unused funds. Such changes usually need to be approved by the funder.

Of course, the best thing to do in the case of underspending is to apply for a timely extension.

EXTENSIONS

An extension is permission issued by a funder to extend the end date for a grant-funded project. Some funders are very easygoing about extensions, and others are not. It is a good idea to find out early how a funder normally deals with extensions so that you will know what to expect as your grant winds down.

If for some reason you were not able to begin serious project work on time (meaning close to the award date), your progress may be slower or behind proposal projections. Whenever any aspect of your project is behind schedule, it is a good idea to investigate and perhaps apply for an extension. Explain the need and reason for the extension carefully and submit it via the funder's preferred method (for example, the National Science Foundation has an online form to request "no-cost" extensions).

When you are exploring an extension, you may be asked for a new end date. Consider the new date carefully and give yourself enough time to get the work done. In many cases one extension is fine, but multiple extensions can become a problem.

REPORTS

Funders generally require reports to be filed at the end of each grant year or at least at the end of the grant period, often 60 to 90 days after the end date of the grant, although sometimes the report may be due before the end of the grant year.

Reports usually consist of a financial section and a narrative, sometimes called a technical report. If the funder provides instructions for the report, follow these carefully. If there are no instructions, prepare financial and narrative reports as suggested below.

The *financial report* accounts for how the grant money was spent and what it was spent on. The financial report is usually prepared by the post-award analyst. Most schools are very good about financial reports; however, it is worth checking with the analyst in advance to be sure she has what she needs to submit the report and that all has been spent according to plan. The minimum report would itemize all expenses and compare them to the total grant, accounting for all funds. Receipts may be required with the report or made available for inspection.

The *narrative report* provides the PI's account of what the grant accomplished. Organizing the narrative report as you would a grant is a good idea, meaning that an executive summary is helpful, as are bullet points, graphs, and tables. Be sure to describe what was accomplished, especially in terms of the promises made in the proposal. Link accomplishments to goals, objectives, and/or benchmarks. Provide information on what the work means to the community. Sometimes letters from community members are appropriate to include.

Submit reports on time, demonstrating once again your mastery of the grant process and your skill as a PI. Some federal agencies will withhold further funding for your project, and possibly for your entire institution, if your reports are very late.

Box 10.4   The Nuts & Bolts: Getting Help With Grant Administration

Grants can turn researchers into administrators. Running a grant-funded project involves many administrative chores, including report writing, budget management, and the management of grant employees. In fact, PIs who resist budgeting for adequate administrative support for major grants can run into problems completing their projects.

One reason this book covers budgets in such detail is to help you carefully consider and predict all the needs that may manifest during project implementation. Major projects may require administrative assistants or coordinators. For projects of over $1 million, this need might

(Continued)

(Continued)

be filled by a full-time employee; however, even ten hours a week of assistance from an administrative assistant who already works part time at the university can provide significant relief to a PI. Assistance with filling out forms, checking time cards, and making basic telephone calls can be a real boon.

Do not hesitate to include reasonable administrative assistance in budgets for medium and large projects. You may be required to document this need carefully in the proposal; however, it will be worth the effort.

WORKING WITH YOUR SPONSORED PROJECTS OFFICE

It is assumed that you are working with your sponsored projects staff throughout the submission, decline, and award process. The sheer magnitude of institutional involvement with awards can be surprising to some PIs, especially in cases where the university did not provide much support during the submission process.

PIs may attempt to accept awards and bear declines on their own, without informing sponsored projects or corporate and foundation relations, as the case may be. It is important, however, to inform university staff whenever you receive a decline or an award. Institutional liability requires this involvement, at least during the post-award period. Because submissions are usually made on behalf of the institution, the institution needs to be informed about their outcomes—especially because a grant may come with requirements that the university needs to comply with.

Of course, some fellowships and consulting agreements are awarded directly to the PI rather than to the institution. When this is the case, the institution should still be included in the following situations:

- When the funding will pay for a course remission
- If the award will provide any funds that would be spent at the university: student workers, wages, copying, and so forth
- When the grant requires that the PI work at the university, using university facilities

The key concept is that if your college or university is involved in some way, then the institution needs to be brought in on the project.

THE NUTS & BOLTS

1. Successful grant awardees often receive many declines. This is because they tend to submit large numbers of proposals.

2. When declined, a PI may receive reviewers' comments, which can help improve future proposals.

3. The award letter usually contains terms, including start and end dates, which are intrinsic to running a successful grant project.

4. Maintaining a positive and open working relationship with your post-award analyst will help to keep the grant running smoothly.

5. Good stewardship of grant funds includes establishing and maintaining good communications with the funder, accounting for all expenses, completing agreed-upon work on time, and complying with the terms of the grant.

EXERCISES: WORKING TOWARD MASTERY

Receive your proposal back from the reviewer (per Chapter 9 assignment) and look at the comments and suggestions carefully. Consider what is being suggested and look for additional errors that the reviewer may not have noticed. Do not limit yourself to the comments of the reviewer—be proactive and honest. Your goal is to make this proposal the best document it can be.

On the basis of this feedback and reflection, revise your proposal thoroughly. Make it better, clearer, and more effective.

If you are using this book as part of a class, submit this revised proposal to your instructor for a grade.

GOING FORWARD

In my time as a grants administrator, I worked with hundreds of faculty, and I edited and submitted hundreds of grants. I saw all kinds of people with various work habits put grant proposals together under a variety of conditions. Sometimes they broke what I thought were hard and fast rules, and sometimes they were awarded anyway. I came in as a successful grant writer, feeling as if I knew the right way to submit proposals. What I learned was that there are countless ways to be effective when submitting proposals.

We have explored at length the many qualities of a successful grant proposal. Grant proposals do not write themselves—the nature of the PI generally dictates the nature of the proposal. In my experience, the qualities of a successful PI include the following:

- **Dedication to getting things right with their projects:** Successful PIs engross themselves in the development of winning proposals and the implementation of important projects.
- **Resilience and consistency:** When successful PIs are declined, they turn around and resubmit. They are generally turned down more frequently than less successful PIs simply because they submit proposals so often.
- **The ability to engender and present useful ideas:** Successful PIs create solutions that are valued by reviewers, funders, and the community.

You can be a successful PI as well, if you work hard, cooperate with your team, and always seek to engender quality outcomes. Successful grant proposals are made of good ideas, good intentions, and the will to create something better—which also happen to be the basic tools for building a better world.

REFERENCES

Eighmy, M. (2009). A trend analysis of manufacturing-related program graduates of community and technical colleges: Great Lakes and Plains regions. *Journal of Applied Research in the Community College, 17*(1), 30–44.

Fairweather, J. S. (2005). Beyond the rhetoric: Trends in the relative value of teaching and research in faculty salaries. *Journal of Higher Education, 76*(4), 401–422.

The Foundation Center (2013). *The Foundation Directory Online, Frequently Asked Questions.* Retrieved from http://fconline.foundationcenter.org/faq.php#13

Gottfried, M. (2012). Career and technical education as a foundation to support postsecondary transitions in STEM for students with disabilities. Unpublished manuscript submitted to the National Science Foundation.

Institute of International Education (2011). *Annual Report.* Retrieved from http://www.iie.org/en/Who-We-Are/Mission-and-Values

Lee, D. N. (2013, January 24). A dream deferred: How access to STEM is denied to many students before they get in the door good. In *The Urban Scientist.* Retrieved from *Scientific American* website: http://blogs.scientificamerican.com/urban-scientist/2013/01/24/a-dream-deferred-how-access-to-stem-is-denied-to-many-students-before-they-get-in-the-door-good/

Malachowski, M. R. (2003). A research-across-the-curriculum movement. *New Directions for Teaching and Learning, 93,* 55–68.

Merriam-Webster (2014). *Merriam-Webster's Collegiate Dictionary* (11th ed.). Retrieved from http://www.merriam-webster.com/dictionary/stewardship

National Center for Science and Engineering Statistics (2014). Academic institution profiles, Johns Hopkins. Retrieved from the National Science Foundation website: http://webcaspar.nsf.gov/profiles/site?method=report&fice=2077&id=h2

National Center for Science and Engineering Statistics (2013). Women, minorities, and persons with disabilities in science and engineering. Retrieved from the National Science Foundation website: http://www.nsf.gov/statistics/wmpd/2013/start.cfm?CFID=9413928&CFTOKEN=47295401&jsessionid=f03088369185bee6076b74576f2a244d215b

Office of Inspector General (2012). *Semiannual Report to Congress.* Retrieved from the National Science Foundation website: http://www.nsf.gov/pubs/2012/oig12002/oig12002_1.pdf

Office of Management and Budget (OMB). (2004). *Circular A-21*. Retrieved from http://www.whitehouse.gov/omb/circulars_a021_2004

U.S. Department of Education (2011). Federal trio programs homepage. Retrieved from http://www2.ed.gov/about/offices/list/ope/trio/index.html

Youn, T. I. K., & Price, T. M. (2009). Learning from the experience of others: The evolution of faculty tenure and promotion rules in comprehensive institutions. *Journal of Higher Education, 80*(2), 205–237.

APPENDIX

Federal Unallowable Costs, the Fly America Act, and Consultants

The federal government awards millions of dollars every year to states, counties, nonprofits, universities, and other entities for activities ranging from studies of human health to the security of U.S. borders. To do this effectively, the Office of Management and Budget (OMB) has established a set of rules regarding grant budgets. For colleges and universities, these rules are described in Circular A-21, Cost Principles for Educational Institutions. The A-21 sets out the bases for costing items in federal budgets, provides guidance in setting indirect costs, and identifies allowable and unallowable costs. Although there is great diversity among the agencies of the federal government, the A-21 helps to maintain unified requirements that make federal granting across agencies similar.

The A-21 regulations may seem intimidating at first; however, they have an internal consistency that can be learned, and they do not change much from year to year. Learning the following basic principles of the A-21 would be helpful:

- Direct costs must be discrete, accountable costs.
- Budgets must only include the costs necessary for the project proposed.
- Taxpayers do not pay for entertainment.
- Unless absolutely necessary, meals are a form of entertainment.
- Federal money cannot be used for donations or for lobbyists.

The A-21 includes a list of unallowable costs (Section J, General Provisions for Selected Items of Cost). These are items that will not be funded by the federal government. Many beginning PIs believe either that including an unallowable cost will cause an automatic disqualification of the project or that no one is really paying attention so these rules can be ignored. Both of these assumptions are untrue.

The federal government puts most of the onus for compliance on the university through the federal audit system. It is true that reviewers, program officers, and other federal grants staff do their best to catch unallowable costs; however, they do not comprise a perfect filter. Most importantly, if a federal program officer overlooks an unallowable cost, this does not mean that the cost has become allowable. Paid-out unallowable costs tend to be caught by auditors and may result in findings against the university. In some cases, these findings can affect the university's ability to continue to compete for federal grants. Careful university post-award officers therefore screen funded budgets for overlooked unallowable costs and may not allow these to be paid out even when they are awarded.

UNALLOWABLE COSTS

There are several categories of unallowable costs. These include but are not limited to the following items.

Advertising and Public Relations

Advertising for the institution is generally unallowable. These costs are only allowed when they are intrinsic to the performance of the project and directly allocable to it. For example, a line item may be budgeted to advertise a project event or to recruit participants for a study.

Alcoholic Beverages

Alcoholic beverages cannot be charged to a federal grant. This is true even when the PI believes that drinks are needed for a project social function, and it means that you cannot have a glass of wine on a travel meal and bill it to a federal grant.

Donations and Contributions

These costs cannot come from a federal award, and further, as nonprofit institutions, most universities seek to acquire donations rather than to offer them.

Entertainment

Tickets to artistic, cultural, and sporting events or for other types of amusement or diversion are not to be paid for with federal grants. Meals are considered entertainment except when they occur as a part of project-related travel or when they are part of a long workday involving partners who have come from a distance. It is useful to think of food as sustenance. Generally sustenance can be charged, while "doing lunch" cannot be charged.

Similarly, potentially entertaining special events are generally nonallowable, including galas, celebrations, receptions, and so forth. One exception is that for certain U.S. Department of Education grants, there may be some latitude for culmination events designed to give participants of instructional programs the sense that they have accomplished something important.

Fines and Penalties

Fines or penalties that might be incurred during the project cannot be charged to a federal grant. Even when related to grant processes, the grant may not pay fines or penalties.

Fundraising

Even for the benefit of the funded project, federal funds cannot pay fundraising costs.

Lobbying

One cannot charge lobbying activities to a grant, even if the lobbying is conducted to further the project.

Materials and Supplies

The budgeting category of supplies is an extremely broad one and surprisingly contentious with federal grants. "Supplies" refer to objects worth under $5,000 per item that are consumed in the course of the project. Science projects may use up chemicals, assays, or syringes. Education projects may use up poster board, pens, and even toys. The contentiousness results from the following criteria:

- Because supplies are items valued at under $5,000, laptops and other electronic items that are commonly thought of as equipment are classified as supplies in federal budgets. This may include video cameras, sound recording equipment, iPads, and so forth.

- In order to be charged as a direct cost, an item must be financially identifiable. One single pencil from a pack of pencils, for example, is not a practically identifiable cost under most circumstances, especially when that pencil sits on the PI's desk and is used for a variety of tasks, including, but not limited to, the funded project. Similarly, the PI's general laptop is not usually chargeable to a grant because it is used in a variety of contexts. When a laptop will be demonstrably and exclusively used for the project funded, it can become chargeable to the grant.

For many PIs, the temptation is to simply add a general line for supplies at some amount, perhaps $5,000, because supplies are not easily distinguishable. The distinguishability of direct costs is important, however. Indistinguishable supplies are indirect costs, and so these are conceptually included in the indirect line.

If what is really meant by "supplies" is poster board and pens to be tracked as separate purchases, then the PI should budget for poster board and pens. Or, if the project will require a significant quantity of copies, perhaps for flyers or handouts, then it is better to add a "print" line, and handle things through the university graphic department so that the cost of the copies will have a receipt and be easily attributable to the grant. Another option is to be assigned a "project only" copy code so that all copies for the grant compose a clearly identifiable cost.

Equipment

The A-21 and therefore federal agencies have a very limited definition of equipment:

"Equipment" means an article of nonexpendable, tangible personal property having a useful life of more than one year and an acquisition cost which equals or exceeds the lesser of the capitalization level established by the institution for financial statement purposes, or $5000. (OMB, 18a, para. 2)

This is a line that appears to be created for large scientific and defense-oriented items, such as electron microscopes and tanks, which are clearly a different class of item than laptops and video cameras.

Equipment needed for the project must appear on the budget and/or be preapproved by the federal agency to be allowable. The best practice is to acquire a formal estimate for the equipment and be sure to consider the costs of tax, shipping, and installation. There are items that are thought of as equipment that are assembled from many "supplies," including specialty experimental apparatuses. In aggregate, this is still equipment and should be estimated and treated as such during the budgeting process.

For the full list of allowable and unallowable costs, see http://www.whitehouse.gov/omb/circulars_a087_2004#1, Attachment B.

OTHER ITEMS OF INTEREST

Fly America Act

For many years, international travelers on federal grants have been required by 49 U.S.C. 40118 to purchase tickets from American flag carrier airlines whenever these are available. This means that even if a foreign airline ticket is less expensive or more convenient than a U.S. airline ticket, the U.S. ticket must be purchased—this requirement is one of the few cases in which lower cost is not necessarily the priority in budgeting. When budgeting, include the American carrier prices, and when buying tickets, particularly to international destinations, call the airline directly and confirm that the journey will follow the Fly America Act. The Fly America Act covers Fulbright awards as well. Be sure to read all of the information available about the Fly America Act because Open Skies Agreements have led to some important exceptions. Go to the General Services Administration website (gsa.gov) and search: Fly America Act.

Collaborators and Consultants

The difference between collaborators and consultants is another topic that can elicit confusion during the preparation of a grant proposal. Collaborators can include co-principal investigators (co-PIs), faculty mentors, and other colleagues who work closely with the PI to plan the project and provide intellectual value to the research. A collaborator shares in responsibility for project implementation and has rights of publication. Collaborators from the same institution are listed on the main budget, and collaborators from other institutions are included in the proposal as part of subcontracts or subawards.

A consultant generally plays a very different role. A consultant is much more like a vendor, hired to provide a specific service that can be easily defined.

A consultant might provide statistical analysis, evaluate a curriculum, or carry out telephone interviews for a survey. A consultant does not have the responsibility of implementation but rather for a carefully defined set of tasks. A consultant does not have rights of publication, because he is not considered an intellectual source of the project.

Table A1

Collaborator	Consultant
Provides original intellectual content.	Provides carefully delineated services (similar to vendor services).
Has rights of publication on the basis of the research.	Does not have rights of publication.
Uses university resources to perform project tasks.	Does not use university resources to perform project tasks.
Typically invests long stretches of time in the project, possibly demonstrated through course remissions and summer stipend.	Typically invests short amounts of time into project, such as a few days or weeks per year.
Effort remunerated through the main budget or a subcontract with the prime.	Effort remunerated on the basis of invoices. Pay is typically for effort of consultant.
Full costed budget, including indirect costs, submitted to prime and to funder.	Estimate of days or hours at standard rate, agreed to in a letter.
Agreement is between institutions.	Agreement is between institution and individual consultant.

INDEX

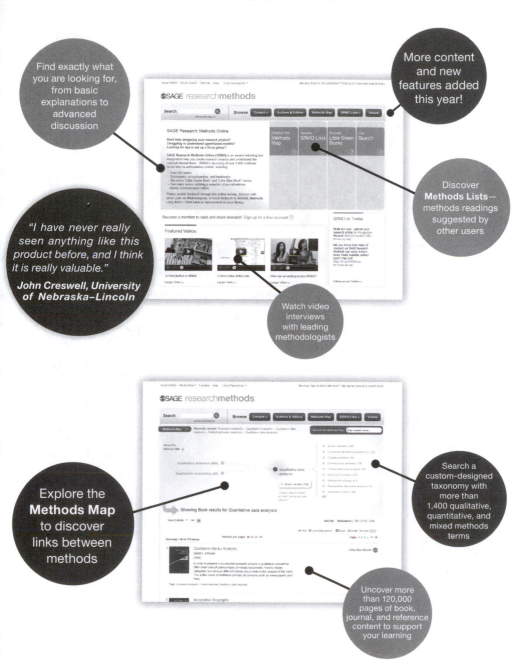

SAGE researchmethods

The essential online tool for researchers from the world's leading methods publisher

Find exactly what you are looking for, from basic explanations to advanced discussion

More content and new features added this year!

"I have never really seen anything like this product before, and I think it is really valuable."
John Creswell, University of Nebraska–Lincoln

Discover **Methods Lists**— methods readings suggested by other users

Watch video interviews with leading methodologists

Explore the **Methods Map** to discover links between methods

Search a custom-designed taxonomy with more than 1,400 qualitative, quantitative, and mixed methods terms

Uncover more than 120,000 pages of book, journal, and reference content to support your learning

Find out more at
www.sageresearchmethods.com